BACK TO BASICS PRESENTS

SIMPLIFY & SAVOR
the Season

ORGANIZE AND RE-ENERGIZE YOUR HOLIDAYS!

BY

CONNIE E. SOKOL

Vyne PUBLISHING

PRAISE FOR *SIMPLIFY & SAVOR THE SEASON*

"In Simplify & Savor the Season, Connie's inspiring stories and practical tips will help you do exactly that. She has a wonderful way of speaking to women's souls, and de-cluttering our minds and hearts."

—Trina Boice, author of *How to Stay UP in a DOWN Economy*

"Reading Simplify & Savor the Season is like getting an early holiday gift: permission to let go of meaningless frills and pageantry and instead, focus on family and love. And it helps the most diehard procrastinators get organized in time to enjoy the holidays."

—Elyssa Andrus, author of *Happy Homemaking: An LDS Girl's Guide*

"Love it! I don't have to hold my breath anymore. Connie is the master at bringing clarity to the chaotic. This book brings to light the little things that make all the difference. I want to tell all women that serenity during the holidays really can happen. What a gift!"

—Kalli Wilson, International Wellness Coach

"Another stellar book by Connie Sokol. Like her other books, Simplify and Savor the Season is filled with wit and wisdom to diminish the chaos of any stressful season, from holidays to family reunions. Connie's step-by-step teaching methods provide easy to use organizing tools to help us de-clutter our plans, feel joy, and create happy memories."

—Fay Klingler, award-winning author of *A Woman's Power: Threads that Bind Us to God*

"Women I talk to are all in agreement of one thing: they dislike the holiday season. Enter Connie E. Sokol's book Simplify and Savor the Season. It's a collection of sensible, easy to follow directions on how to focus on the family while keeping the season simple. This book is a must-read, especially before the craziness begins."

—Valerie Steimle, Book Reviewer and blogger

"Connie has sprinkled her trademark humor throughout this insightful, and much needed, book. She helps lead the reader through an easy 3-step plan that will simplify the holidays and yet keep what is dear to your fa mily. This book helps remind the reader to stop, breathe and wonder at the holiday magic."

—Taffy Lovell, Book Reviewer

ISBN: 978-0-9890196-2-0

Published by Vyne Publishing, Woodland Hills, Utah

Table Of Contents

To my fabulous family and friends,
and women who through the years—and life experience—
have taught me to simplify and savor
so I can focus on the good.

Acknowledgments

❋   ❋   ❋

This book came to fruition only through incredible timing, insights from dear friends, and help from a gracious God above. And, on a pragmatic note, a happily sleeping baby. Without his helpful naptimes, this book would not exist.

To my wonderful family who shares with me in myriad ways each literary journey, and allows others to glimpse highly personal moments of our lives in order to help them move forward in theirs. I love and adore each of you beyond expression.

My to-the-bone-thank-you to Jodi Robinson who, at pivotal times, talked me down from the ledges and gave me perfect insights in just the right doses. To my writing group for their spot-on suggestions and motivational yet helpful feedback. And to those wonderful women whom I can randomly email, asking for opinions on covers, titles, or even doo-dads, without offense. I'm so grateful for your kindness and expertise.

As always, my gratitude to the behind-the-scenes women: my excellent editor, Kelley Konzak; my faithful formatter, Heather Justesen; and my graphics genius, Kelli Ann Morgan. Without these talented, helpful women, this book "simply" couldn't happen.

And to you lovely readers whom I possibly haven't yet met but always feel a close connection to. As women, wives, and mothers we already have so much in common that my writing and your reading creates a sort of meeting of the souls. Thank you for making time for that experience in your life.

Best,

Connie Sokol

INTRODUCTION

It's that magical time of year that we women do amazing, awe-inspiring, migraine-inducing things to make sure our loved ones enjoy this special season. And we hope that we will get to experience this joyful time, or remember how wonderful it truly was.

To illustrate, I share this excerpt received from a friend years ago that had circulated on the Web. It's written by an applicant to New York University who was required to write an essay on any significant experiences or accomplishments that would influence the university staff as they considered him or her for admission to the college. The person responded with the following:

"I'm a dynamic figure, often seen scaling walls and crushing ice. I have been known to remodel train stations on my lunch breaks, making them more efficient in the area of heat retention. I translate ethnic slur for Cuban refugees, I write award-winning operas, and I manage time efficiently. Occasionally, I tread water for three days in a row.

"...My deft floral arrangements have earned me fame in international botany circles. Children trust me. I can hurl tennis rackets at small moving objects with deadly accuracy. I once read *Paradise Lost*, *Moby Dick*, and *David Copperfield* in one day and still had time to refurbish an entire dining room that evening. I sleep once a week; when I do sleep, I sleep in a chair.

1

"The laws of physics do not apply to me. I balance, I weave, I dodge, I frolic, and my bills are all paid. Years ago I discovered the meaning of life but forgot to write it down. I have made extraordinary four-course meals using only a mouli and a toaster oven...I have played Hamlet, I have performed open-heart surgery, and I have spoken with Elvis. But I have not yet gone to college."

And though no name appeared, it was noted that the author of the post had been accepted and was attending NYU.

Why do I share this vignette? Because for me, this is *exactly* how the holidays can feel. The season becomes chaotic and crammed, and I face an impossible level of multi-tasking as I balance, weave, dodge, and frolic from activity to experience, and still get the bills all paid.

Let me be clear on one thing from the start: the holidays are stressful *not* because you and I lack extreme juggling talent. Quite the opposite. They are stressful because society will not let women sit down for five full minutes and be unproductive. It's because the details of executing the holidays continue to change, multiply, and morph, depending on the number of children, extended family, and drop-in neighbors that fill your home. And, of course, it's because department stores continue to move up the floor show on "BE PREPARED FOR THE HOLIDAYS—BUY NOW" to start sometime around Valentine's Day. This can squeeze any potential holiday cheer from the season.

Many years ago, with four children—ages six and under—and all the attendant shopping, diaper changing, placating-crying-children-*while*-shopping-and-diaper-changing, I changed my overriding Christmas list of what I wanted to "get" to two things: to get the whole thing over with already, and to get back to sleep.

Teen years didn't make it that much easier. Suddenly concerts, social outings, and dances (never mind needing more *creative* ways to ask someone to said dances) were jammed into an already packed schedule.

It was too much.

Finally, while the last measure of pre-season sanity remained, I devised a plan. This included a truly *simple* holiday planner, a few principles to stay focused, some humorous journal entries, and a bar of good European chocolate with hazelnuts.

Success.

Using this same plan, now I yearly and honestly *look forward* to the holidays each year. In fact, even while writing this book, my excitement for the coming season has already begun! No longer do I approach October through January with hesitation or even rabid fear. With a few simple but doable changes, I've reclaimed the joy of the holiday season, and so can you.

If the thought of facing down the holidays has you curled in the fetal position, worry not, this handy holiday book is for you. Not only does it give you the 3-Step holiday planner (which no sane woman should be without), in the "Simplify" section, but after completing your holiday plan, you can also put your feet up, let your hair down, and enjoy the humorous but helpful holiday columns in the "Savor" section.

Simple, organized, enjoyable. And that's how we do that.

PART ONE: SIMPLIFY THE SEASON

A Word of Christmas Cheer...

Before we begin our fabulous 3-Step Holiday Plan, let's first lay the emotional groundwork for a successful season. If you begin to feel anxious, overwhelmed, and possibly in despair—and it's only July—then you're not alone. For many women the mere thought of organizing gift-giving makes them want to move to small towns in Peru.

The good news is that with a few simple coping skills, you can avoid the holiday rollercoaster of emotions.

In *Faithful, Fit & Fabulous* I share the need for Joy Juicers—behaviors and perspectives that actively but simply create more happiness on a daily basis. As you apply one of the following holiday Joy Juicers in your own time and way, it can replace that often burdensome feeling surrounding the season with a new peace, hope, and love

5 Holiday "Joy Juicers"

1. Focus on a feeling. At the risk of sounding too Hallmark Theater, consider ahead of time this question:

What feeling do I/does my family want to experience and remember the most this holiday season?

We all have different expectations of the holidays, and generally, what we hope for is a kind of feeling—that once-a-year tingly anticipation of something magical in our lives.

The particular feeling you and your family want isn't as crucial as being intentional about it. Choose a feeling that fits your needs or desires: peaceful, exciting, joyful, or spiritually grounding. What matters most is that you choose what matters to you.

Once that "feeling focus," is decided, it's simply about planning activities accordingly. A few years ago we wanted a more meaningful family Christmas. We wanted to forego attending holiday activities pinball style. You know what I mean: "Ping goes the ball, off to Aunt Myrtles, stop at the Christmas Tree Festival, hurry to the toy sale, help at the school cake walk, race to husband's work party, come home and drop into bed, ball goes down the hole, start again tomorrow...Ping goes the ball..."

Instead, we did it differently. We *focused* on creating a few simple experiences that would specifically relate to uniting and strengthening our family, both our living and our ancestral families.

The result was this: We discovered and completed a little more family genealogy; I scrapbooked our current family pictures (current, meaning within the last five years); we recorded memorable moments in a holiday journal; we connected with family, both present and past, through religious worship and activities, and we spent many evenings together playing games, watching old Christmas shows, and doing simple crafts.

I don't think any of my children would say it was an amazing, incredible, never-to-be-forgotten Christmas. But in a subtle but tangible way, we *felt* more connected to each other and to our forebears. When I think back on that Christmas it feels good, warm and meaningful—and that's without every single minute being devoted to the endeavor. Focusing on a feeling doesn't mean every single activity will exactly fulfill it, but as we choose intentionally, we experience more purpose and depth.

2. Involve the family. The holidays are for *family*, so let them help. Let go of your inner controlling Mrs. Claus, and understand that even she uses elves (I have it on good authority). When everyone pitches in, each can enjoy the experience and you can let go of the *Mom Show*. Not only is that a gift here and now for you, but it is also a future gift for your children, because they will use those life skills year after year and be prepared them to be stellar adults (and relieve your holiday stress).

In a beautiful illustration of this, religious leader M. Russell Ballard shared that it takes about 20,000 to 60,000 bees to collect one pound of honey (or prepare the annual Christmas cards—I've heard it both ways). That means, on average, about one-twelfth of a teaspoon per bee. But then he said, "Work that would be overwhelming for a few bees to do becomes lighter because all of the bees faithfully do their part." ("Be Anxiously Engaged," Ensign, October 2012.)

As we involve each family member and his or her one-twelfth of a teaspoon, and then add our Wise Mother and Orchestrator of Many Christmases Past one-twelfth of a teaspoon, the experience is more meaningful for everyone. During different life seasons of motherhood we will obviously add more than one-twelfth of a teaspoon (more like half a pound). What matters is that each member receives an opportunity to use his or her talent, ability, or enthusiasm in the celebrations.

3. Keep it simple. Especially during the holidays, conventional wisdom encourages women to consciously assess and reduce their expectations, because emotional and physical overload can create "yo-yo" emotions. Too much to do combined with the desire to please too many people can create a lose-lose situation.

Coping skills such as such as saying no, properly prioritizing, or being a little more bold about your needs are vital. Years ago I was asked to help prepare an activity for young girls. I don't quite remember the theme or what the girls experienced, but I do remember the preparation. Not only did copious meetings precede the event, but also, the night of the activity the leaders apparently had been assigned to bring most of their home furnishings, and possibly those of their neighbors. Many lamps, chairs, and tablecloths adorned the room while delicate tea edibles were stacked on matching tea trays, accompanied, of course, by coordinated napkins, cups, and handouts.

The girls were eight to twelve years old.

Sure it was a stunning sight. But it required more planning and set up than a wedding reception. And as I said, I don't remember the actual theme.

So the point here is, to keep it simple. Ask yourself:

Am I doing this to create family memories, or for show?

Am I making this because I love my family, or to check it off the list?

Am I being present in the moment and enjoying this event or am I thinking ahead to when it will be done, or planning the next thing?

Consider how much holiday stress you'll eliminate by focusing on those who matter most and not on how someone might perceive you or your item, event, or decor.

Joanne Larsen, author of *I'm a Day Late and a Dollar Short*, shares the experience of a woman who was asked to bring "a few pies and a vegetable tray" to a holiday party. Wanting to really shine, she handmade six pies, and instead of a simple vegetable tray, made a veritable vegetable forest, including shaped miniature mushroom and broccoli trees. Ultimately, she was so exhausted that she couldn't even attend the festivities!

4. Acknowledge the highs and lows. Holidays bring such grand expectations that we're automatically set up for crushing disappointments. I believe that's why funny holiday movies make us able to laugh at the inevitable highs and lows.

In the classic movie, *A Christmas Story*, Mr. Parker has a series of perpetual disappointments—his daily battle with the Oldsmobile engine freezing up; his "Major Award" lady's leg lamp that is "accidentally" broken by his wife; and his constant annoyance at the invading next-door neighbors' dogs. The ultimate insult comes on Christmas Day, when the dogs steal into the kitchen and drag away his favorite—*the Christmas turkey.*

The narrator says, "The heavenly aroma still hung in the house. But it was gone, all gone! No turkey! No turkey sandwiches! No turkey salad! No turkey gravy! Turkey Hash! Turkey a la King! Or gallons of turkey soup! Gone, ALL GONE!"

Our family actually experienced a similar situation with a Christmas ham and our dog named Ginger. Let's just say she didn't make the Good List that year...

This is how celebrations can feel—It's ruined! With so many events and activities, some major disappointments are bound to be part of the package. For the next three months, life will be notched up 300 percent with additional visiting family, back-to-back parties, children's concerts, and a gift list so large you could use it for wallpaper. There's a reason why this is considered the most stressful time of year, particularly if you experience seasonal affective disorder (SAD).

Validate the shift in life and possibly mood. Recognize life got busier, with less time to accomplish the tasks, and that to combat sudden feeling spikes, high or low, you need more conscious, consistent positive drops in your emotional bucket.

At Healthy.com, twenty-five experts recommend very doable tips for de-stressing the season. I've included just a few here.

✳ Put a drop of lemon or orange essential oils on your wrist or hanky to smell throughout the day (research shows it helps with depression by increasing norepinephrine).

✳ Get some sunlight by sitting near a window.

✳ Calm your mind and body with a brisk walk during the day or a natural relaxation supplement at night to decrease anxiety and increase serotonin.

✳ For a quick tension release, press the fleshy place between your index finger and thumb (called the *hoku* spot in traditional Chinese medicine) for 30 seconds.

✳ Laugh to reduce stress and improve your immune system.

(For more, you can www.health.com.)

Try one or two this holiday season, to relax and rejuvenate. I triple dog dare you.

5. Keep the spirit of the season. I saved the best for last. Amongst the variety of religious celebrations during this time of the year, for many, the ultimate reason for the season is the birth of Jesus Christ. Weaving a spiritual focus through your celebrations will truly make the difference in your holiday season, creating a more fulfilling and bonding experience with family and friends.

Religious leader President Thomas S. Monson says, "Christmas is what we make of it. Despite all the distractions, we can see to it that Christ is at the center of our celebration. If we have not already done so, we can establish Christmas traditions for ourselves and for our families which will help us capture and keep the spirit of Christmas." ("Because He Came," Christmas Devotional, 4 December, 2011.)

Many cultures remember His birth in wonderfully unique ways. In Greece they eat christopsomo, or "Christ Bread." The crusts of large sweet, various-shaped loaves are decorated in unique ways that denote the family's profession. And in England, the day after Christmas is called "Boxing Day." Years ago people donated to the poor through church alms boxes. On December 26, in similitude of the Savior's service, the boxes were distributed to the poor. Nowadays, people often give small monetary gifts to their mail carrier or news vendor.

No matter the specifics, the more you involve Jesus Christ throughout the season, in a *personally meaningful way*, the more deeply fulfilling it will be.

For our family, we've done a variety of things to focus on Christ. Like most families, we read the Nativity—either at one time or incrementally through December—and act it out on Christmas Eve. We watch movies, read books, and religious talks on who the Savior was and is, and how His teachings help us today. In trying to be like Him, we enjoy giving anonymous gifts, serving and donating at charities and projects, and sharing at the dinner table about our "Daily Do," which is a spontaneous service.

To make Christmas more meaningful to me individually, one December I daily posted on my website a thought on a character trait of Jesus Christ. After receiving requests to compile the complete set of posts, I created a seasonal devotional book, *40 Days with the Savior*, sharing His character traits and how they related to my life as a woman, wife, and mother, and added a thought-provoking question for each day. I also donated the profits to a community food bank. For me, this experience created a layered connection to Him. I felt peaceful because writing the small book was part of my study and an enjoyable medium of expression. I was able to give back in a small way, and, it daily kept Jesus Christ forefront in my mind and heart during both the Christmas and next Easter season.

Whichever way you choose to celebrate the reason for the season, add something meaningful about the Savior. The spiritual brings the substance—the tinsel adds the twinkle.

There you have it, five doable and enjoyable "Joy Juicers" to prepare for and sustain your holiday happiness.

Now, let's simplify the season.

Now that we've prepared for an emotionally healthy holiday, let's continue to simplify and savor with the 3-Step Holiday Plan.

Your 3-Step Holiday Plan—It's a Family Thing

This shockingly simple planner helps you clearly list the needs and to-dos of the season, in one place, and to clarify the right amount of "energy to task". This means, only applying the necessary amount of time and energy to an event or to-do, instead of cluttering it with unnecessary frills or details.

Though the planning sheet looks as simple as your kindergartner's homework, I beg you not to complicate it. Sure you can tweak, tailor, and enhance it, but definitely *keep it simple*. This pared-down plan helps you lose HPP (Holiday Planning Paralysis) while motivating you to intentionally choose and enjoy a positive seasonal experience for your family.

You can create this holiday plan in three steps: Brainstorm (5–10 minutes), Family Buy-In (30–60 minutes), and Detail (10–15 minutes). All in all, it's fast, fabulous, and fun.

Let's get PADE!

To complete the plan, we'll use the PADE formula, which stands for Plan, Abbreviate, Delegate, and Eliminate.

PADE: PLAN

The first step is to identify which activities, events, and experiences are most important to you and your family. Then, to organize all planning information you need to plan for them—what to do, buy, decorate, make, and so on—in one easy-to-find spot. Let's start by jotting down thoughts about what makes your family celebrations meaningful.

Untouchables and Enjoyables

Consider your holiday feeling focus from the Joy Juicers section. Then, think about your traditional events or activities. What are some of the "untouchables"—meaning, those traditions that you *must have* to make it *your* family celebration? Maybe it's creating hand-made ornaments, doing a New Year's piñata, or making Aunt Martha's fruit cake. Whatever core family traditions make it special for you and your family, list and prioritize them below.

Then list some of the "enjoyables"—the items that would be fun *if* they work with the schedule. Maybe a spooky corn maze, a new holiday concert, or a local holiday festival.

You can do this exercise first by yourself to become familiar with it, and then invite your family to do it, too.

Untouchable	Enjoyable
-----------------------------------	-----------------------------------
-----------------------------------	-----------------------------------
-----------------------------------	-----------------------------------
-----------------------------------	-----------------------------------
-----------------------------------	-----------------------------------

Finished listing a few on the columns above? Fabulous. Now use your Untouchable and Enjoyable lists to specifically brainstorm a plan for all four holidays: Halloween, Thanksgiving, Christmas and New Year's. Don't make this overwhelming, it's a fast overview. You can use the "Brainstorm Holiday Plan" worksheet provided, or a computer screen, or the back of one of your kids' old homework papers. (All planning pages are available in a companion *Simplify & Savor Take-Along* at www.conniesokol.com).

Simply list the four main holidays evenly spaced across the top: Halloween, Thanksgiving, Christmas, New Year's. Down the left hand side, list the categories you typically use during the holiday seasons: Decorations, Food, Gifts, Travel, Activities, Events (activities with a set date and time), and so on. Leave about an inch or two per category so you have room to add more or leave notes.

YOUR 3-STEP HOLIDAY PLAN:
Master Brainstorm Page

	HALLOWEEN	THANKSGIVING	CHRISTMAS	NEW YEARS
DECOR:				
FOOD:				
GIFTS:				
ACTIVITIES:				
EVENTS:				
TRAVEL PLANS:				

Let's do it!

Set the timer for one minute and brainstorm the *main* events, items, and to-dos you already know will be part of the first upcoming holiday. Use the listed categories or create your own. For example, for Halloween it might look like this:

YOUR 3-STEP HOLIDAY PLAN:
Brainstorm Page

	HALLOWEEN	THANKSGIVING	CHRISTMAS	NEW YEARS
DECOR:	Decorate on family night Buy new decorations			
FOOD:	Chili and cornbread on 31st Make rice krispie skeleton hands for school party Pumpkin bread for breakfast the week of			
GIFTS:	Buy Halloween candy			
ACTIVITIES:	Pumpkin patch Our hom Halloween party Trick or treating Cookie decorating for family night			
EVENTS	Halloween Parade at the school 10/31 @ 2:15pm			
TRAVEL PLANS:	Visit grandparents Monday before Halloween			

Let's do it!
Now that you can see how one holiday might look, **set the timer for one minute per holiday** for the others and quickly complete the categories underneath each one. Remember, this is only brainstorming! No need to feel that planning paralysis or to enter every detail. You're simply *getting down the basics* and will add more detail later.

TIP: As you enter events and items, try to keep a slice of the planning pie free for whatever joyful surprise drops in your lap. This is the magic. An impromptu caroling fest for the neighbors? Helping a family move in on Christmas Eve? Whatever it is, you'll remember it more than your very carefully laid plans, so leave a little intentional room for the X factor—as in eXciting and unexpected—to make it a memorable holiday.

That's it. You now have a rough blueprint of your master holiday plan. Can you believe how easy that was?

Before you go to the next phase of *detailing* the first upcoming holiday, it's ideal to involve your family with their thoughts and feelings. Because these are family celebrations, the family members should have an active part in the planning process, if for no other reason than this: to get the family "buy-in."

Step 2: Family Buy-in

Too often women feel solely responsible for creating a successful holiday season, but when we involve our families, they feel more joy, create memories, and learn life skills. To do this takes getting the buy-in—meaning, holding a semi-official meeting to ensure that with time, energy, and enthusiasm, they will put aside electronics to help hang the holly wreaths.

Right from the start, hold a family night to invite their ideas and opinions. Begin just as you did in this book, by covering the five Joy Juicers and then choosing together a feeling focus. After that, ask everyone to share their "untouchables" and "enjoyables," with someone acting as the scribe.

Last, make it a game! Use the 3-Step Holiday Planner template, set the timer for five minutes per holiday, and let the children shout out their favorites in each category. Don't include detailed to-dos—this will lead to boredom and a possible marshmallow fight. Then together, narrow down each category to the most important traditions per holiday—generally about three to five—so everyone is on board with what matters most. Wrap up the evening with a fabulous family treat and get giddy about the coming fun.

Step 3: Detail the Plan

Once you have the family's input on the holiday plan, merge that with your own. From here, you'll add in the Mother Knows Best details—the backstage, unseen kind that help the holidays function. Use the Detailed Holiday Plan worksheet shown here to more fully lay out each holiday. Some require more planning than others: for many, Halloween can often be done a week ahead, while for others, Christmas prep may start in mid-October. (All planning pages are available in a companion *Simplify & Savor Take-Along* at www.conniesokol.com).

Let's do it!

Set the timer for five to ten minutes and *for only the next upcoming holiday*, complete the detailed categories of Do, Buy, Call, etc. Make it helpfully detailed, which means don't list minutiae you would likely accomplish anyway. List instead the to-dos that are easily forgotten or weigh on your mind.

DETAILED PLANNER BY HOLIDAY:

POSSIBLE CATEGORIES: Decorations, Food, Gifts, Travel, Activities, Events (set date and time), Service, Other--or fill in your own!

DO:							
BUY:							
CALL:							
OTHER:							

For example, your "Detailed Holiday Plan for Thanksgiving" might look like this:

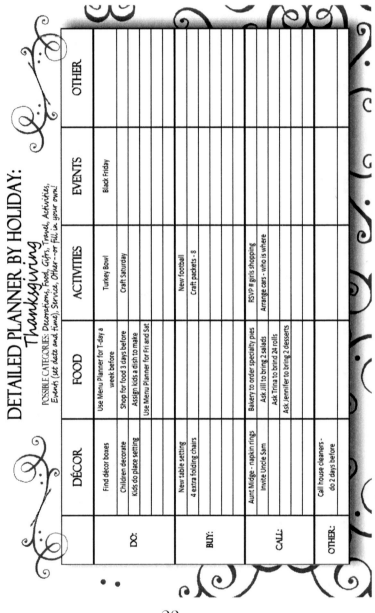

DETAILED PLANNER BY HOLIDAY: Thanksgiving

POSSIBLE CATEGORIES: Decorations, Food, Gifts, Travel, Activities, Events (set date and time), Service, Other – or fill in your own!

	DÉCOR	FOOD	ACTIVITIES	EVENTS	OTHER
DO:	Find décor boxes Children decorate Kids do place setting	Use Menu Planner for T-day a week before Shop for food 3 days before Assign kids a dish to make Use Menu Planner for Fri and Sat	Turkey Bowl Craft Saturday	Black Friday	
BUY:	New table setting 4 extra folding chairs		New football Craft packets - 8		
CALL:	Aunt Midge - napkin rings Invite Uncle Sam	Bakery to order specialty pies Ask Jill to bring 2 salads Ask Trina to bring 24 rolls Ask Jennifer to bring 2 desserts	RSVP # girls shopping Arrange cars - who is where		
OTHER:	Call house cleaners - do 2 days before				

The Final Plan

You've brainstormed and then detailed your first holiday. Great job! Look it over and consider how it feels. If you love it, fantastic—you're finished. Go straight to the "Savor the Season" section and enjoy humorous columns on surviving and thriving through the holidays.

However, if you're feeling as though the plan is already too much, seems confusing, or is overwhelming, continue to the next section on how to easily de-clutter the plan, keeping only what is core to you and your family.

One thought on the final plan: Remember, you're the mom, which means you are the one who will be driving, baking, calling, and in all ways making this holiday plan fly. Once the family has decided what's vital, then you spearhead the how-to, asking for input but reining it in when it gets out of control (without, of course, being tyrannical, obsessive, or overbearing. Ish.)

Why do I say this? Because sometimes family members aren't aware of the layered requirements that lurk behind certain activities. To them, most of the celebration to-dos can seem either minimal or really fun: "Why can't I build a life-size replica of the nativity out of candy canes?"

Help them understand that as the mom, you understand what goes into it and therefore, you need to set healthy boundaries on what will ultimately be best for the family's well-being as well as yours. Otherwise, you might feel compelled to please, then overschedule, and then feel resentful, when your family won't know what went wrong in the first place.

As the saying goes, "If the mama ain't happy, ain't nobody happy—if the papa ain't happy, ain't nobody care." Because it will be the mom who is barking at children and slamming cabinet doors out of frustration after having decorated a hundred miniature gift stockings for the school party until 4 a.m.

21

De-clutter Your Holiday Plan

If you've gazed upon your Detailed Holiday Plan and suddenly feel the need for a paper bag to breathe into, let's use the remaining steps of the PADE formula to get a little clarity.

PADE: ABBREVIATE

Abbreviate is another word for simplify. In order to enjoy the season in a realistic and paced manner, we need to trim what isn't essential; mainly, because this is the *start* of the season. Expect it to continue to inflate.

But sometimes it's hard to see what to cut out. In the live action movie, *How the Grinch Stole Christmas!* the Grinch faces this same problem. He says: "The nerve of those Whos. Inviting me down there—on such short notice! Even if I wanted to go, my schedule wouldn't allow it. 4:00, wallow in self-pity; 4:30, stare into the abyss; 5:00, solve world hunger, tell no one; 5:30, jazzercize; 6:30, dinner with me—I can't cancel that again; 7:00, wrestle with my self-loathing. I'm booked. Of course, if I bump the loathing to 9, I could still be done in time to lay in bed, stare at the ceiling and slip slowly into madness. But what would I wear?"

Sometimes we also get a little Grinchy when we pack in too much play—and of course, try to decide what to wear.

So how *do* we appropriately decide what stays and what goes?

Carolyn J. Rasmus says in her book *Simplify*, "To simplify is about enhancing our ability to focus on things that really matter, to deliberately choose our priorities, and to refuse to let unimportant things take over the things of real importance."

That's the key—focus on things of real importance and then choose wisely. I mention in a story in the "Savor the Season" section about a visit from my out-of-state mother one

22

Thanksgiving. On the agenda was taking a trip to the dinosaur museum, making gingerbread houses, eating a homemade dinner, and more—and that was just the first day! With this ridiculous schedule I ultimately discovered one important point: everyone actually wanted to play games and be in pajamas. So we cut, cut, cut and brought back the joy.

Here are some specific ideas for cutting out what might be crowding your holiday plan.

Abbreviate activities. Choose one holiday on the 3-Step planner and read through it, and select one activity or task that feels overwhelming. Ask yourself, what is the *energy to task* needed for this? That is, ask yourself, how much energy this *requires*, instead of how much you would *typically apply*. Without "putting on a show" and instead, creating memories, how can you simplify the activities and still create the feeling you desire?

For example, each year our family makes gingerbread houses, as I mentioned above. But for me it was becoming a bah-humbug. Even though we used the store-bought houses, they were huge, the icing stuck to everything but the gingerbread, the children fought over who could decorate what, and the clean-up time was more than it took to decorate them (which is saying a lot). Then, like an old fake reindeer in the yard, the houses would sit there, twisted and petrified, and might I add, taking up precious counter space.

The solution? Smaller houses. Genius! We found *mini* gingerbread houses, five to a box. Everyone chose their own house, the icing stuck better on a smaller space, and all five houses easily combined into a decorative scene. Instead of a three-hour tour, we finished in just over an hour with time for games and cocoa. Humbug who?

Let's do it!
Set the timer for one minute and choose *one* activity to abbreviate.

Abbreviate gift-giving. Whether you scurry online or frantically store-hop, consider seriously shaking up your gift giving. Ask yourself:

What are the most stressful aspects to gift-giving for me?
What would make gift-giving more enjoyable?
How can I do one thing differently this year to make it so?

To de-stress this aspect, consider alternating years of gift-buying with Memory Makers, donations, and service opportunities.

Memory Makers. For these experiences, take the money you would have spent on each other or extended family and put it into a memory-making experience such as a vacation or service mission. Time spent together as a family is typically more memorable than the gifts each child received (with the notable exception of the official Red Ryder Carbine-Action Two-Hundred-Shot Range Model Air Rifle, with a compass on the stock and a thing that tells time...)

As a family, we've foregone the focus on presents and instead, went sledding at a cabin in Park City, Utah, enjoying yummy slow-cooker meals and snuggling in a Sound of Music—like down comforter. We've played tennis in St. George, Utah, going out for Chinese food a la *A Christmas Story* on Christmas Day. And we've body-surfed the waves in San Diego, California, enjoying a gorgeous sunset on Christmas Eve. This year, consider making a memory instead of a purchase.

Donations. Rather than give extended family members yet another furry hand muffler, try making a donation to your or their favorite local charity. Often the big-name causes receive more focus while the local ones are overlooked. Support a local food bank, coat and blanket donation center, or homeless shelter and get connected to your communities.

To top it off, make homemade family cards to share what you've donated and a little bit about the charity. Sometimes we also send a yummy representation of our state, such as local nuts, fruit, or honey. Beautifully, the needy are given relief while your family gets more connected in doing good.

Service opportunities. If you're ready to notch up the service even more, perhaps make a service opportunity the only Christmas gift. Several of our friends participate in yearly service building or community help missions to foreign cities. They take their families for a few days up to two weeks and build houses, create irrigation, teach gardening, and more.

Some friends of ours who have participated in one such program, Builders Without Borders of Utah (www.builderswithoutbordersofutah.org) shared this experience:

"For the past few years our family has celebrated Thanksgiving by travelling to Tijuana, Mexico with a group of friends to build and repair homes for impoverished people there.

Each year, we have arrived thinking of all the good we will do in this poor, famished border city. And each year we leave Tijuana having received more than we could ever give.

"We have made friends there that we will never forget. We see kindness, happiness, and patience from people who live in plywood, pallet, and corrugated metal homes. We see the people of this culture as real people, as individuals with families and lives and hopes and dreams, and so we understand and accept better those not of our ethnicity. We don't see these people anymore in stereotypical fashion or lump them together. Instead, they are our neighbors and friends.

"Explaining what our Tijuana adventures have done for our family is impossible. The closeness we've gained, the refocusing of priorities we've experienced, and the love for humankind that's been enlarged in our hearts is a miracle I hope every person will get to experience at some point in their lives."

In any travel situation, choosing a safe, reliable and well supervised program is important. Through careful choice and planning, this can be a life-changing, inexpensive gift that can strengthen family bonds.

Let's do it!

Set the timer for one minute and choose *one* way to abbreviate gift-giving. Ask for or share your idea with your spouse and other family members.

PADE: DELEGATE

Choose a category in your holiday plan that stresses you out. As you read over it, consider this question: "If I were bedridden, had a heart attack, or experienced a sudden paralytic episode, what could I delegate?"

The answer, of course, is all of it.

I remember my friend telling me about a time when her family was moving to a new home. She was on bed rest for a pregnancy and her husband had just sustained a hernia. The two of them were literally on the bed giving instructions to the neighbors, who moved every last thing in their house!

The key to delegating is to enjoy the process—no uber hovering, dumping, or complaining. For example, one year I looked at our holiday plan and decided to delegate what I had previously tackled by myself in this way:

The Christmas tree. We set the actual tree up as a family and then gave the children decorations and one instruction—lights and pine cones go first. They did a stellar job (with a few charming gaps here and there...) while I made tasty victuals and Dad tried to get the lights to work. Now they happily decorate the tree each year.

Gift-wrapping. I realized that people love gifts wrapped in bizarre and unusual ways *as long as it's done by children*—what would be odd or offensive from you is considered "absolutely darling" from them. If that's too much for OCD you, take a large roll of white poster paper, let your children put their hand prints in various paint colors on it, and let it dry. Voila—cozy, children-made wrapping paper.

And older children are fabulous Christmas Eve Santa's Helpers, especially for Really Old Elves who have a hard time staying up past 9 p.m. As the children have matured, we've loved this aspect because while wrapping we can laugh over old memories, watch favorite Christmas shows, and generally get it right who is to receive what.

Easy neighbor gifts. Don't feel the need to make a production of neighbor gifts. For an easy-to-assemble present that the children could make, we paired a can of gourmet cocoa with a large jar of almond biscotti and tied them together with festive ribbon. Fast, fabulous, and kid-friendly, it was a perfect combination. We even caroled for the neighbors when we stopped by to give the gift. Of course, no need to mention the postcard experience of the children fighting over who could sit up front, which carol to sing, and whose turn it was to give the gift...

Family newsletter. As you know, any fifteen-year-old can do a better job on this happy holiday tradition than adults can. So let them! To simplify, I took my own advice and put one child in charge of typing and printing, and the others over folding, stuffing envelopes, labeling, and stamping. We delivered them to the neighbors with a carol (repeat "postcard experience" from above), and finished at home with cocoa and a Christmas show—a perfect family night.

Remember, this is not abdicating holiday responsibilities or dumping to-dos on everyone else. Not at all. It's allowing everyone to feel part of the process.

Let's do it!
Set the timer for one minute and choose one activity or item to delegate. Share it with your husband and family or, better yet, get their opinion on how to do it!

PADE: ELIMINATE

Lastly, as you consider your holiday plan, how does it feel and look to you? Still too busy? Not focused on the feeling you're going for this year? If abbreviating and delegating isn't working, then simply eliminate it. Remember, it's just for this year, so you can eliminate an event, activity, or task that isn't working for your family *for one holiday season.* If you've *always* made Christmas doilies for all thirty-five of your neighbors but this year the very thought gives you hives, *then don't make them.* Traditions are meant to bind us together with love, not make us want to beat each other with knitting needles.

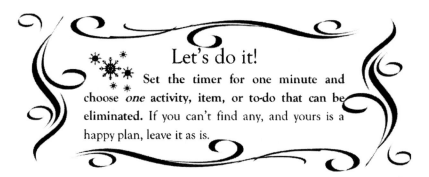

Let's do it!
Set the timer for one minute and choose *one* activity, item, or to-do that can be eliminated. If you can't find any, and yours is a happy plan, leave it as is.

You're done!

Using the 3-Step Holiday Plan, you've both personally and as a family chosen a feeling focus and listed untouchables and enjoyables. You've brainstormed the needs for all holidays and detailed a plan for the next upcoming one. Applying the PADE formula, you've de-cluttered what isn't essential and focused on what is.

Your 3-Step Holiday Plan is finished. Can someone say glad tidings of great joy! Sit back, relax, and enjoy a Danish butter cookie.

What to do now?

Post your 3-Step Holiday Plan on a family board, or write in the specific events on your family calendar so everyone is on the same page. One year, for example, from October through December, I wrote one main event and one main to-do on the big calendar in large bold letters each week. This also created a timeline of what to expect.

Each successive week showed one to-do item: Week 1—Decorate the house. Week 2—Prepare and deliver newsletter. Week 3—Buy Gifts. And each week listed *one main event*. Week 1—Christmas Concert. Week 2—Secret Santa. Week 3—Neighbor caroling. We consistently knew what was most important to us and we didn't feel overwhelmed by it.

Use a Menu & Helper Planner, and Simplified Gift List

This section is optional and only if you find it helpful! If you want to further organize and re-energize your newly simplified holidays, consider these two additional helps.

Menu & Helper Planner

While serving a mission in Japan for The Church of Jesus Christ of Latter-day Saints, I spent New Year's Day with a wonderful Japanese family. They taught me something I still use and love. To celebrate New Year's, many Japanese people spent literally all day cooking and eating. This Japanese family kept it organized by listing the menu and then leaving a blank line next to each dish. Each of us got to choose which meal we wanted to help prepare.

Fantastic! Instead of one person in the kitchen all day, or too many people at once, this easy format made it fun and functional.

If you don't have a menu and helper plan already, use this very simple planning sheet for a basic but handy menu plan to combine with your 3-Step Holiday Plan.

Menu & Helper
PLANNER BY HOLIDAY

	ITEM	GROCERY LIST	SOUS CHEF (HELPER)
APPETIZERS:			
MAIN DISH:			
SIDE DISHES:			
BREAD/ROLLS:			
DESSERTS:			

	KITCHEN SET		HOUSE PREP
SET THE TABLE:		CLEANING DETAIL:	
TIDY THE KITCHEN:		LAUNDRY:	
CLEAN UP AFTER DINNER:		HELPER:	

And if you need a one-stop organizer for gift-giving, jot down your notes on this Master Gift List. (All planning pages are available in a companion *Simplify & Savor Take-Along* at www.conniesokol.com).

MASTER GIFT LIST:

POSSIBLE CATEGORIES: Family, Extended Family, Neighbors, Teachers/Coaches, Kids, Friends, Church, Community—and Others!

WHAT?							
BY WHEN?							
NEED TO DO:							
NOTES:							

A Note on Maintaining a Happy Holiday Plan

Now that you've finished your plan, you face the actual onslaught of the holiday season. How do you keep your fabulous schedule from hyperexpanding like a post turkey dinner stomach?

Very simply: when you agree that the family schedule still makes everyone look forward to the holidays rather than dread them.

As the season progresses, be aware of how you and your family generally feel (not obsessively—it is the holidays and you are a family, after all). If there is consistent anger, resentment, or anxiety, it's likely time to go back and apply a little abbreviate, delegate, or eliminate.

Congratulations! Before you opened this book the holidays were a vague, stressful, amorphous mass of expectations pulsating in the corner (think 1950s, *The Blob*). Now, you've got a plan and your family is on board!

Remember that the most important part of any holiday celebration is to *be present and enjoy the experiences with those around you*. A plan is meant to be a helpful tool, not a rigid requirement. As you approach the holiday season with more organization and awareness, you will be able to let down and let go, enjoying all the surprise, wonder, and joy the seasons can bring.

"And the angel said unto them, Fear not:
for, behold, I bring you good tidings of great joy,
which shall be to all people."
Luke 2:10

PART TWO: SAVOR THE SEASON

If you asked many mothers what they ultimately wished for the holiday season, what would they would say? What would *you* say? Aside from a personal assistant, perhaps it would sound something like this Dear Santa letter that circulated on the Web:

"Dear Santa,

"I've been a good mom all year. I've fed, cleaned, and cuddled my children on demand, visited the doctor's office more than my doctor and sold sixty-two cases of candy bars to raise money to plant a shade tree on the school playground.

"I was hoping you could spread my list out over several Christmases, since I had to write this letter with my son's red crayon, on the back of a receipt in the laundry room between cycles, and who knows when I'll find any more free time in the next eighteen years.

"Here are my Christmas wishes:

"I'd like a pair of legs that don't ache (in any color, except purple, which I already have) and arms that don't hurt or flap in the breeze, but are strong enough to pull my screaming child out of the candy aisle in the grocery store.

"I'd also like a waist, since I lost mine somewhere in the seventh month of my last pregnancy.

"If you're hauling big-ticket items this year, I'd like fingerprint-resistant windows and a radio that only plays adult music, a television that doesn't broadcast any programs containing talking animals, and a refrigerator with

34

a secret compartment behind the crisper where I can hide to talk on the phone.

"On the practical side, I could use a talking doll that says, 'Yes, Mommy' to boost my parental confidence, along with two kids who don't fight and three pairs of jeans that will zip all the way up without the use of power tools. I could also use a recording of Tibetan monks chanting 'Don't eat in the living room' and 'Take your hands off your brother,' because my voice seems to be just out of my children's hearing range and can only be heard by the dog.

"If it's too late to find any of these products, I'd settle for enough time to brush my teeth and comb my hair in the same morning, or the luxury of eating food warmer than room temperature without it being served in a Styrofoam container.

"If you don't mind, I could also use a few Christmas miracles to brighten the holiday season. Would it be too much trouble to declare ketchup a vegetable? It will clear my conscience immensely. It would be helpful if you could coerce my children to help around the house without demanding payment as if they were the bosses of an organized crime family.

"Well, Santa, the buzzer on the dryer is calling and my son saw my feet under the laundry room door. I think he wants his crayon back. Have a safe trip and remember to leave your wet boots by the door and come in and dry off so you don't catch cold.

"Help yourself to cookies on the table but don't eat too many or leave crumbs on the carpet. (You promised me last year you would lose some weight with me so next year you and I could be a cute, size two blonde...OK, some requests go too far, but none the less...

"Yours Always,

"MOM

"P.S. One more thing...you can cancel all my requests if you can keep my children, healthy, safe and of course, young enough to always believe in Santa." ["A Dear Santa Letter from Mom, author unknown.]

Would some of this make *your* Dear Santa list?

Barring new legs or kids that don't fight, what will make this season more wonderful than previous ones is our ability to truly *savor* it. Unfortunately, too often the day-to-day grind collides with the one-time expectations and suddenly, moms are left holding the bag—or the to-do list—and reducing the holidays to no more than a series of dreaded tasks.

Once we've carefully prepared our lists, home, menus, and more, it's time to focus on the experience! To *savor* the events, activities, and meals rather than snow-blow through them. If we don't, we will be just another stressed-out mother armed with a shopping cart.

In the Webster Dictionary, to savor literally means to "appreciate fully; enjoy or relish." Doesn't that sound delightful? I want to "relish" the experience of a Thanksgiving full of family, memories, and delectable food. I want to "appreciate fully" my children's enthusiasm on Christmas Eve as they act out the Nativity with thrown-together costumes and then gather beneath the tree, taking turns reading from *A Christmas Dress for Ellen*.

Savoring the season means more of being still, looking people in the eyes, and connecting with them in the moment. It's truly tasting that scrumptious tart, from start to finish, tingling your tastebuds with delight. It's putting the video camera down and fully watching your daughter sing her solo with all the accompanying nervous facial tics (have your son do the taping). And it's sitting on a cozy couch by a chilly window, as you watch the falling snowflakes to the snowy ground.

Savoring is reclaiming the magic of the season, to experience a mature version of what our young children instinctively feel, as found in this quote from *The Polar Express*.

"At one time, most of my friends could hear the bell, but as years passed, it fell silent for all of them. Even Sarah found one

Christmas that she could no longer hear its sweet sound. Though I've grown old, the bell still rings for me, as it does for all who truly believe." (Chris Van Allsburg, *The Polar Express*, Boston: Houghton Mifflin; 1985.)

If you've forgotten how to savor—to soak in the magic and beauty before you—then try a few of the following brief "Savoring Suggestions." One or all can help you reclaim your ability to savor, which is, of course, best accompanied by a cup of warm, frothy cocoa.

1) Pause and pray. With the backdrop of such family and faith-based holidays, it's ideal to take a few moments during the day to breathe in and out, and feel grateful for what you have and who you are. As Maya Angelous says in *Celebrations: Rituals of Peace and Prayer*, "Let gratitude be the pillow upon which you kneel to say your nightly prayer."

Gratitude is such a small but powerful and simple thing. While driving, it's easy to think of three things to be thankful for. When sitting down to dinner, ask your family for their thoughts on the subject. At our family dinners we let each child share a high and a low (or two highs) about their day. Suddenly, what seemed to be a fairly tough experience turns out to be a pretty sweet day after all.

Whatever you're doing—cooking, shopping, cleaning—pause for thirty seconds for a prayer of gratitude. Whatever the reasons, big or small, you'll find the season to be more fulfilling.

2) Record meaningful moments. Yes, it's a busy time of year—but a beautiful one to sit by the quiet, low-lit Christmas tree at night, maybe with a cup of cocoa (stop worrying about calories) and to record meaningful moments with your family, friends, or even random strangers. Write down grateful thoughts, wishes, or hopes for yourself and your family. Record lovely observations like pretty snowflakes or the stillness of the world.

In *A Christmas Carol*, author Charles Dickens writes of Scrooge, "He went to the church, and walked about the streets, and watched the people hurrying to and fro, and patted the children on the head, and questioned beggars, and looked down into the kitchens of houses, and up to the windows, and found that everything could yield him pleasure. He had never dreamed that any walk—that anything—could give him so much happiness." (*The Best of Short Stories of Charles* Dickens New York: Charles Scribner's Sons, 1947.)

The real happiness lies in the small but meaningful observations.

My family has a holiday journal in which we write "funnies" or special experiences. (Let me clarify "write": the last entry dates back three years). One of our favorite entries is when my daughter tested the Thanksgiving mashed potatoes one year. "Are they hot enough?" she asked as she literally stuck her finger into the bowl. Then howling with pain she pulled her finger back out.

Yep, they were hot enough.

Even now when we bring out the mashed potatoes someone is likely to ask her, "Are they hot enough?" Whatever seems of worth to record, serious or silly, jot down a few memorable moments to enjoy now and in the future.

3) Seek service. As we age, Christmas can inadvertently lose some of its sparkle. Some feel awash with increased stimulation, high expectations, and bitter disappointments. Others feel as if they're on a holiday conveyor belt of singing the same old carols, eating the same old treats, and getting the same old gifts, only now it's on warp speed.

To recapture the magical feeling, seek spontaneous service. Create moments that not only bring joy at the time, but that you'll also remember and feel warmed by for years to come.

One of those moments happened for me at a post office. As I stood in line—miraculously sans children—I noticed an elderly man standing at a counter, looking dazed as he stared at a mass of envelopes and papers before him. I approached him and asked if he needed help. He turned to me with a sort of lost expression and said, "My wife just died, and she always did the Christmas cards."

This sweet man was obviously hurting and overwhelmed. So I took a few minutes to help him get things sorted and prepared. It didn't take that long and I didn't do anything particularly amazing, but I can still remember that warm, full feeling of helping this man in his need.

4) Let go of the Cookie-Cutter Christmas. It's hard to say it, but sometimes we women are our own worst enemies during the holidays. Mostly because we want everything to be cozy, beautiful and, well, perfect.

It *will* be, if we *let* it be. As in, if we *let* the events and people unfold and enjoy without choreography, it will be perfectly imperfect. Mishaps and mayhem—these create the keeper moments that we'll laugh and reminisce over. This is the unexpected magic that binds us together.

One year we were doing our Secret Santa, which involves leaving an anonymous money gift on a person's porch. In stealth mode late at night, our family slowly drove in a mini-van around the cul-de-sac and dropped off the two "Helper Elves." Then we drove down the street so as not to attract attention and, after enough time to ensure they made the drop, made our way back to pick them up. As we approached the house, we could hear our two kids crying *incredibly loudly* outside the family's front door. After adjusting our eyes to the dark we realized what had happened—the family's sprinklers had come on and soaked our already chilly boys (which begs the question, who has sprinklers on in December?) We still laugh about that experience. Remember, it doesn't have to be a Currier and Ives picture to be a meaningful moment.

5) Look to a new year. As you savor the season you're in, know that another wonderful transition is around the corner. Not in a go-go, need-to-plan-ahead way but more of an exciting anticipation that a fresh new year will be here soon. What do you want to become, do, feel, see, and experience in the next year? Enjoy it for what it is: a clean slate and a moment of pure possibility.

H. Jackson Brown, Jr., quoting his mother, said, "Twenty years from now you will be more disappointed by the things you didn't do than by the ones you did, so throw off the bowlines, sail away from safe harbor, catch the trade winds in your sails. Explore, Dream, Discover."

Open your mind and soul to those new possibilities, jotting down the thoughts, dreams, and direction that come. Then when the new year rolls around, you'll already have a seedbed of ideas for a fruitful year.

Use these "Savoring Suggestions" when you start to feel a bit frazzled or too functional, and enjoy the next section of humorous thoughts and essays to put your feet up and take a load off.

You're finished!

Remember that the holidays are a swirl of emotions and activity. As you use this small but useful book, you can simplify the organizational details of each celebration. And, with that structure in place, you can enjoy the unfolding of each event or activity.

Simplify and savor—these are both surefire ways to make a meaningful holiday season no matter what specific events, people, or situations may be involved.

SAVORY SNIPPETS

A collection of short holiday thoughts

Loose Change That Changes Lives

If you've read *Christmas Jars* by Jason F. Wright you'll know it's the story of a girl who, hours after her apartment is robbed, mysteriously receives a jar full of change and random currency. Being a reporter, she is suddenly alerted to many other people who have also received this same simple but timely money jar gift, with some of the jars containing as much as five hundred dollars.

We have such a family jar into which we have thrown loose change throughout the year, though not exactly equaling five hundred dollars... After reading this book we decided to give our jar anonymously in our traditional doorbell-ditch Secret Santa delivery. The excitement that abounded in our children from exhibiting stealth that rivaled the pounding of small African elephants was beyond description. And we can only imagine what these wonderful people might do with approximately $72.50–in change. But still, the point is, we were out there, serving, and pawning off our loose change.

If you've been wondering what service to do this year, consider decorating an old canning jar and scavenging the house for random coins. You'll discover the simple joy you can pass on!

Doing the Kind Thing

On a particularly run-run-reindeer kind of day, I raced through a grocery store with my son for needed food-stuff and then hurried to the car to make it to our next stop on time. After stowing the cart, we were about to leave when a woman literally came *running* toward us.

"Did you just put a cart away?" she asked.

I hadn't, but my son had, so my first thought was, "Whose car did we hit?"

Instead she said, "I think your wallet is still in there."

What a woman! She had no idea what that meant to me—that because of the day's schedule I likely wouldn't have realized the wallet was missing until the following day, when I would be seriously low on gas and would likely not realize that either until the telltale slow-and-stop of the car. Her considerate few minutes saved me a possibly frazzled day.

In this vein, Amanda Dickson shares in her book, *Wake Up to a Happier Life*, about the importance of taking a moment to do a kind thing, even if it's only to say thank you. She was at Costco getting chicken enchiladas, and as she reached in to retrieve them, she saw the woman who likely had made them, wearing a hair net and an exhausted expression. Amanda mouthed, "Thank you," and wonderfully, this woman immediately experienced a shift in her countenance.

A well-lived life really is about the little things: taking three seconds to smile, letting the car go ahead of you, thanking the salesperson for excellent service. These courtesies are what make our days soft and round, and take the edge off of seemingly endless to-dos. Look for the love, do the kind thing, and bask in the joy.

Disconnect from the Get Button

One Christmas we broke the exciting news to our children that Santa had sent a *personal email to our family.* Shazam! In fact, it was in *direct response* to our personal email sent to Santa asking him to "bring something this year that would help us create family memories rather than focus on things."

"What a great idea!" we said. "And look," we added, "Santa also said that to help us create memorable family time and eliminate materialistic tendencies, our family was to receive an *all-expense paid trip to sunny St. George, Utah for Christmas. And,* if the children were all extra good, they would each receive *one present!*"

Breathless, we looked to our children and anticipated their response. My oldest daughter burst into tears. "But I'll miss the snow!" she wailed and refused to be consoled. My eldest son looked contemplative: "Does that really mean *one* present, or does that only apply to the little ones?" And, unable to let it be, he pestered me again days later for further gift details, adding that, hey, maybe he could buy one extra gift for himself...just in case. In a tender teaching moment, I told him, "You know, son, this is a great experience because regarding materialism, those who struggle the most will learn the most."

He looked at me dazed and uncomprehending, but I felt better.

In all fairness to my children, they whine less than the average teenagers and are openly grateful about shiny things. But we do feel that this experience will be just what is needed to disconnect from the "get" button. What will *not* happen on Christmas morning is kids shaking boxes and elbowing for what's potentially theirs, or sequestered at their computers, XBox, or friends' houses. No, we will be compelled into family bonding (let it begin), playing board games (I can feel the stress already), and swimming at the hotel daily (possibly twice a day). And mom and dad will come home in traction.

Thank you, Santa. Our Christmas wish come true.

In Need of Holiday Laughter

The other day my husband and I exchanged with old friends joyful experiences of raising rambunctious children. My husband shared a time when he and our son were working together at a job site, and how our son had, out of curiosity, inventively and expertly stuffed a large wad of cotton clear up into his nasal cavity. After my son finally confessed that he couldn't get it out, my husband attempted to retrieve it but without much success. My son was a bit cavalier about the whole thing, which only added to the frustration of his father.

Then my husband said that in order to get the cotton, he would have to use a drill bit and carefully reverse it out.

Then it got really interesting. My husband continued his story: "I pulled over my work van, none too happily, and started chucking stuff out of my tool boxes to find the right size bit. Fear had obviously hit him because suddenly, I could hear him up front, sneezing hard and fast to get the cotton out before I came back."

Hearing that story and seeing the imagery made me laugh out loud, right from the toes. And it felt freshly fantastic.

Have you laughed today? Have you had a snicker, chuckle, or an all-out belly guffaw? If you want a bit more family unity and joy, try laughing together. The Mayo Clinic verifies that laughter relieves stress, stimulates the heart, releases endorphins, soothes tension, improves your immune system, acts like a painkiller, increases personal satisfaction, and decreases depression and anxiety. (See http://www.mayoclinic.com/health/stress-relief/SR00034).

Wow. If that's the case, maybe a few pages of *The Far Side* or a favorite download of Bill Cosby might be the ticket for a stressed-out soul. Just for today, find something to laugh about, and when you do, write it down. This may be the most important prescription you follow.

Holiday Keeper Moments

Recently, I had one of those lovely keeper moments while driving with my two little ones and my fourteen-year-old son to set up a booth for an event. To be honest, early that morning as I considered the day ahead, feelings of avoidance and exhaustion ebbed and flowed; frankly, I didn't feel like doing what needed to be done.

But driving with my sweet children, hearing their chatter, and viewing their fresh faces in the rearview mirror, I changed my tune. Like a fresh gust of wind, instead of focusing on the "dreaded to-dos," I simply focused on the day with my children.

That changed everything.

Suddenly, we were on an adventure. We were heading on a "trip" to Salt Lake, having lunch at Cafe Rio, and being allowed to run wild in the huge event warehouse without getting into trouble. Beyond the play, my son unrolled the large awkward carpet—with suggestions on how to situate it—and my four-year-old delighted in being a "helper".

As we drove home from a thoroughly enjoyable day, I experienced a waterfall of peace and joy start from my head and cascade all the way to my toes, causing me to spontaneously say, "I just love being with you guys."

Attitude is everything. If you have an event or activity that feels a bit too much, instead of dreading the to-dos, consider the day as a whole, with all the beauty, joy, and relationships you can wrap it in.

Thankful for Warbling

One year my kindergartner was chosen to represent her class in the Turkey Warbling contest (i.e. make sounds like a turkey). This was no small honor (so much so that one of my sons who was *not* chosen took some coaxing to *let it go* and move on with his life).

From start to finish, this was a lesson in being thankful for the little things: hearing her practice last night with great seriousness and technique; watching her courageously "compete" for the free turkey; and noting how the dedicated judges deliberated for a full five minutes with a requested redo because it was *such a tough choice.* We finished off with pictures of my daughter standing tall and proud next to our kind principal who was bravely dressed as a turkey, complete with red tights.

I'm so thankful to be a part of life's little things, the moments that make up the days of my family, husband, friends, and plain good people. Because it's truly those "little things" that are the big things in creating joyful, fulfilling lives.

Thankful for Pivotal People

Years ago I read a book called "Five Wishes" by Gay Hendrickson, who shared how one vital conversation had changed his life.

As I thought back on conversations, and moments, like that in my life, and the people who made them possible, I was filled with gratitude.

My first thought ran to my sixth-grade school teacher Miss Lynda Hatch. She was the one who took interest in me during a turbulent period in my family life. Her leadership, confidence and high expectations helped cement my desire to do good and be my best. Because of her caring and extra attention—allowing me to grade papers afterschool while munching Oreos—I chose to obtain my degree in teaching and have desired to teach in some form most of my life. Miss Hatch, who went on to win various awards including Teacher of the Year, saw something in me that I couldn't yet see in myself, and helped me to catch the vision.

That's a pivotal person.

What a gift we give each other when we say or do the right thing at the right time, often stepping out of our comfort zone to say or do it. Today, I encourage you to list three names of such "pivotal people" in your life. Then I invite you to contact one of them and let them know how much you appreciated their influence. Although my search for Miss Hatch proved unsuccessful, I am trying to express my thanks by leaving a hopeful influence in my own teaching.

Thankful for Resealable Bags?

As I approach this Thanksgiving holiday, and in an unexplained rush of great gratitude over the weekend, I made what seems to be a slightly unusual list of things that I appreciate.

After the usuals (family, home, Danish butter cookies) I pondered the overlooked yet supernally meaningful items—things such as . . . resealable bags. I love these things. In my soul I believe these were invented purely for me, and I use them every day of my life to containerize vital items such as crumbly cereal, hardware we'll never use but can't part with, or wipes that my daughter has pulled out—one by one—from the baby wipes bag.

And while we're on that very subject, baby wipes! *Where* would I be without them? They clean everything my children can conceive of dirtying. And, when our city lost water for a week we did baby wipe baths until house water was restored.

On and on the gratitude goes, from car seats, to email, to cheap legal note pads, we are surrounded by fabulous inventions and doo-dads that make our lives that much better.

Granted, these undervalued items may not rank with the emotional stir of birthing a baby, but the usefulness of these inventions can truly bring a grateful, "ahh." Consider a few unusual items you appreciate and quite possibly, you'll be filled with a bit more holiday gratitude.

Simplify to Stay Sane

Due to my mother's upcoming visit for Thanksgiving one year, I stopped at one of those superstores the size of a small state for a few fresh groceries. As I navigated my cart through the aisles, and was reminded somewhat of the running of the bulls at Pamplona, at every turn I met women with furrowed brows and stacked carts, threatening fisticuffs to get their frozen turkey first.

Before I gave in to the get-mine-first war, a beautiful realization suddenly dawned on me: I did not need to compete! Two weeks earlier I had completed my handy dandy 3-Step Holiday Plan. Using this simple device I had decided and purchased in advance what was vital for dinner, a decidedly low-key affair. As in bass low-key. As in turkey, potatoes and gravy, two veggies and rolls. That's it. Finito. Leftovers included.

With this joyful knowledge, I fairly skipped past the fistacuff ladies and moved forward with the confidence of knowing that the bulk of my meal shopping was complete. This left me free to experience a creative surge, a notion to actually purchase those nice dishes that I had desired for years: Chili red ceramic plates with golden chargers and Tuscan yellow dessert dishes. It was a sign. (Later, after setting the holiday table, my son looked at it and said it actually resembled a work of art. My holiday was made.)

If you're feeling the frazzle, use the 3-Step Holiday Plan and spend more time chilling instead of barking. Or fighting over frozen turkeys.

A National Change

In Stephen Covey's book *The 8th Habit*, he shared a story about the late Anwar Sadat, president of Egypt and how his ability to radically change his way of thinking ultimately changed a nation.

Sadat had been a politically popular, die-hard anti-Israelite, going so far as to vow never to shake the hand of an Israeli. Then suddenly, at least to his allies, his fundamental thinking shifted.

He realized he was wrong.

Can you imagine the political fallout from such an admission? But, determined to do the right thing, Sadat made an historic trip to Israel, even while facing possible death from political fanatics. Braving this endeavor successfully, he returned home to hundreds of thousands of people lining the streets, cheering him and supporting his choice. Many of them were, ironically, the same people who cheered for him to never go.

This is a beautiful time of year for us to reflect on our beliefs and our behaviors, even our very course of life. Mr. Sadat shared, "He who cannot change the very fabric of his thought will never be able to change reality, and will never, therefore, make any progress." (Stephen R. Covey, The 8th Habit: Free Press, New York, p.56)

What thoughts will you change this coming year? What joy will you embrace, and what negativity will you let go? Change requires courage, to see who we are and who we can become.

And this kind of change begins by choosing one belief or behavior, and acting on it today.

What Determines Life Satisfaction?

If you're feeling in need of a little help to face the new year, consider the advice from Dan Zadra's short but stylish book "5."

He shares to "Start by choosing the two most important 'guiding stars'—your values and your mission. [Then] create goals to help balance the wheel of your life. Think of your life as a wheel with many different spokes. To have a balanced life, each spoke needs your attention." (5, Seattle: Compendium, 2007, p.5).

If you're married with children, that's a lot of spokes. But happily, there's no need to be overwhelmed. Instead, use your values and mission to stay focused on what's core despite the possible mayhem that will preside. This will bring ultimate daily peace and confidence, and the knowledge that you're aligned with what you believe to be paramount.

Ironically, when comparing the life satisfaction level of Forbe's 400 richest Americans, those of the Inuit people of Greenland, and the cattle herders in Kenya (living in dung huts with no electricity or running water), *the level of life joy was the same.*

This year, consider what matters most to you and put your *best* energy into those areas, starting with just *one* area. Begin with a clear focus, apply appropriate energy, and build on the outcome. If it's weight loss, begin with an eating or exercise program that truly resonates with you. Then wisely begin, starting slow and reasonable until aspects begin to be your lifestyle. Last, build on your success by rewarding your efforts and reviewing your vision. Bit by bit, you will balance the beautiful spokes on your life wheel.

Getting Unstuck

As you face the thought of January, I invite you to open your mind and soul to your unique talents and abilities. Rather than staying mired in daily minutiae, how can you best use those gifts this coming year? What are projects or creations that you've yearned to attempt but haven't?

And if you haven't, why not?

So often we desire to branch out in our lives, to feel the energy of doing something bold, but we're afraid—of failure, embarrassment, lack of knowledge or expertise, or just plain afraid. But you can share yourself and talents with others at any age, and in any way that reflects your core values, goals, and personal inspiration.

At age twenty-one, Fred DeLuca co-founded Subway with just a thousand dollars in savings, and at age seventy-eight Grandma Moses *started* painting. In 2005, three college kids wanted to share videos online with their friends. So they dabbled and devised a simple invention—a way for virtually any video to play on any web browser. They began their own company called YouTube. A year later they sold it to Google for 1.6 billion dollars and their idea was named Time magazine's Invention of the Year.

Gear up and let's go. This year, dig deep and discover your personal talents to share with the world.

# SAVORY STORIES

A collection of humorous holiday experiences

Keeping Christmas "Time"

A few years ago I attended an incredibly large religious conference with a few other religiously inclined women. Up front we had been advised to be in our seats by 6:30 p.m. or we wouldn't be able to attend. With the event an hour away, we religious women wanted to be on time—it wouldn't do to show up late or not be permitted in at all—and made sure that carpool arrived right on time.

Except for one woman—there is always one in the crowd, after all. Right from the start, she seemed oblivious of the vital seat advisory, much to the dismay of the rest of us type A's. After she delayed the car pool at her house by half an hour (and no explanation!), we chose to forgo enjoying dinner that evening and instead, with ticking minutes to spare, hurriedly entered a nearby food court and each ordered a pizza slice to go. This, with the intention that everyone would, of course, eat it on the go.

However, this sweet but tardy gal chose to order a pasta dish and then *sat down to eat it*. After exchanging discreet but distressed looks between our watches and each other, most of us sensibly edged toward the food court street door as a sure signal for her to *move it along.* Not a few were becoming frustrated at her obvious disregard for our seating urgency.

And then, an incredible thing happened. Right at the apex of our watch-checking, one of the lesser type A ladies kindly said, "It's okay. I'll stay with her."

That person was not me.

Relieved to be freed from the hold up, the rest of us hurried on, like so many busy ants, to attend our *religious* meeting.

I can honestly say that I felt a few tugs at my heart, pulling me to this kind woman and her example, and to the teaching of the moment. But I'm embarrassed to say that I punctually deferred these heart tugs until later because *we had to be in our seats by 6:30 p.m.*

Practically power walking in our Sunday dresses, we finally arrived at the conference hall, out of breath and just in time, but only to find out that you could indeed be seated *after* 6:30 p.m.

There we stood, each of us feeling appropriately guilty, until the other two ladies arrived, both with a clear conscience (one from lack of awareness and the other from doing the right thing).

In this hurried holiday time, I invite you and me to remember that a kind service is the right thing to do, even if we fear it will—perish the thought—make us late. In the end, I do believe we will be right on time. The kind of time that matters.

How the Real Halloween Fright Happened the Next Day

The other night was hysterical, in a certain sort of way. At the end of a busy Halloween night, we returned home, and immediately my sweet husband was out like a light (he'd been up at 4 a.m. for several mornings in a row and had enjoyed the dulcet sounds of our baby's opinion on nighttime teething). Thinking to be the good wife, I decided to let him sleep while I spearheaded the rest of the family. After all, Halloween was rapidly coming to a close.

How hard could that be?

At 10:30 p.m., in my pajamas, my son tells me I need to drive his friend home—not down the street, mind you, but to a neighboring city. I returned just as our sixteen-year-old came home from his party at 11 p.m. but then stayed up to tell me *all* about it until almost midnight. At 1:30 a.m. the baby woke up with, you guessed it, sore teeth, and an opinion on it. At 2 a.m. my nine-year-old entered our room saying and gesturing that she was throwing up, not from candy, I discover, but from swollen glands.

At 3 a.m., and just as I get her settled, my seven-year-old entered our room with, we discover, swollen glands also, but with the bonus of a fever. At 4 a.m. the baby wakes again and by this time, I can't keep track of who is slee--ping where and who needs what. At 6:30 a.m., after a few stolen hours of shut eye, my seventh-grader wakes me up and tells me she doesn't feel very good.

Didn't Thomas Paine once say, "These are the times that try men's souls?" I think he got that from his wife.

On the upside, the next day was spent with all my sick children cuddling on my big bed, watching a show, or playing some quiet Skip-Bo. By the end of the day all was made right.

But what I learned from the memorable experience was this: next Halloween, I'll be prepared with medicine, apple juice, and a take-a-number format for The Nightmare after Halloween but Well before Christmas.

Thankful for the Unexpected Gift

A few years ago—to be specific, the day after we took our eldest son to college and my youngest had started first grade—I found out that I was pregnant.

With our seventh. At age forty-six.

That was a tough day. Not from a lack of loving children—I fiercely adore my own, and love the children I randomly meet at church, in the neighborhood, or generally anywhere as long as I don't have to check their homework and make sure they brush their teeth.

It was the motherhood difficulties that immediately crowded my mind. And I'm embarrassed to admit that the first was not the health of the baby, but how much weight I would gain. I'd just lost a good amount from the last child, had kept it off, and was finally feeling I no longer had to think about how to squeeze three feet of muffin top into two inches of waistband.

But on the heels of that vain thought was the reality of what we could expect at my age. Down syndrome, chromosomal issues, trauma to my body—these were tangible concerns, and that was just the beginning. I also had six other children at home, my oldest with Asperger's syndrome, and each child needing their own particular care at any given time. Then came the thoughts of late night feedings, diaper changing, car-seat lugging, and the dreaded potty training.

Suddenly, life looked hard.

But then something amazing happened. Little Bryson was born. And with that incredible, overwhelming, joy-filled event, there went every single, solitary concern. Seeing that beautiful, healthy eight-pound-fifteen-ounce baby, my heart opened wide and wrapped him up. Every day since then I thank my Heavenly Father for this incredible, sweet-tempered, unexpected gift.

I can't explain all that his presence does for me and our

58

family. At church, we look down the pew and see our children quietly barter to hold him, passing him from lap to lap after their appointed time. My sixteen-year-old burps him right there with the cloth over his shoulder on his suit coat (which I realized that he realized makes him a chick magnet). Bryson's sweet nature and calm demeanor have profoundly affected all of us. It's lessened the loudness of our home and the bickering between siblings (to a degree), and improved the general caring for one another. He provides a sort of gathering place, a tangible hub where everyone instinctively meets. He is our new family connector, as we all initially come to give him a squeeze, a kiss, or a coo, and in the process connect with each other as well.

For myself, I'm shocked that my worries all came to naught. And, in considering the difficulties of a late-in-life baby, I hadn't allowed for the intangible gifts and unseen help that come as a package deal to make the whole experience magical and normal at the same time.

So this month, I invite you to consider, and even share, an unexpected gift you have received in your life. And hopefully feel again the wonder of what you didn't know could be.

Thankful for the Unexpected Joy

A short while ago, my friend and author was telling me about a fabulous week-long writing conference in a city four hours away from us that she was to attend. After I shared my happy response to this, she suddenly stopped mid-sentence and said, "You should come."

My first instinct was to say, Wow, sounds amazing—*have a good time.* Because there was no way I could take a week off, last minute, in November, with *seven kids.* And yet, some nagging part of me kept blurting out questions—who, what, where, when, and would there be chocolate?

Then reason took over. Obviously, I said, it couldn't work because I would need to bring my baby. To which my friend said, Bring him. Wow. Then I thought about the seminar instructor— a national author in the biz for over 20 years—who would surely not feel the same. So I emailed him (why not?) And he said, Bring him. Wow.

Then I checked the family schedule—surely, it just wouldn't work. Unbelievably, the calendar was barely full, needing at most two carpool switches. That's when my friend threw in the kicker and said, Stay for free at my relative's house. Suddenly, this experience looked very doable. Lastly, I ran it by my husband who said, Do it. And, as a bonus and to include couple time, he would drive down to meet me for a weekender after the conferences.

Wow to the tenth power.

And so I went. Not without unbelievable choreography such as reviewing with my children the schedule, their life skills, and awesome rewards for stellar behavior (and ominous warnings of no computer games for those without). I kissed them goodbye and loaded up my friend's compact car, stuffed to the windows with baby stuff and writing supplies.

What an incredible experience. Ironically, due to my son's teething I ultimately didn't attend the daily morning classes, but I didn't stress. Instead, we spent the week playing together, mother and son, taking him for walks while he was awake and writing feverishly while he napped.

Throughout the week my friend and I discussed what she'd learned, talked plot lines and characterization, and supported each other in our writing goals. While holding these writing chats, my little one happily played next to me without being hauled in and out of a car seat with the go-go of kids' routines.

Quiet, peaceful, sacred time, that's how it felt. And to top it off, like something out of a novel itself, my husband drove four hours through a bitter raging winter storm to see me and our baby for the weekend.

Between my friend's lovely invitation and generous friendship, the writing growth and accomplishment, my husband's fabulous appearance and time spent together, and our eventual sweet reunion with amazing children who had actually cleaned, cooked, and kept up their home routines, it was an overwhelming, unforgettable Week of Joy.

So here is my grateful expression for the unexpected joyful gift, and my deepest prayers and hope that when life gives you such a joyful gift, that you'll prayerfully open your heart and go with it.

Thankful for the Unexpected Memory Maker

My mother came to visit for Thanksgiving. As I thought about the fabulous traditional things we wanted to do with her, I happened to see a Knit/Crochet Kit at a store. Ironically, that very thing had been on my mind: to have this amazing, multi-generational experience of Mom teaching my girls (and reminding me...) how to knit.

I thought back to my knitting days (a long, long time ago in a teen galaxy far, far away...), and the hideous tan-colored scarf of my first attempt that was about six feet long and three feet wide. Though it was never worn—what a shock—it could have doubled as a tent canvas.

Back to modern day, on a cozy fall afternoon five girls of three generations pulled out the craft kit and we all set about talking, laughing, and knitting together.

BEST. DAY. EVER.

Truly. My girls, ranging from 13 down to 7, caught on quickly and with a little encouragement (and some better needles), did wonderfully. Because I had stopped at a local store for various yarn choices, each chose their favorite color and got to it. Not only did they enjoy Grammie teaching them how to cast on or avoid dropping a stitch, but they kept at it on their own. I can still see the picture in my mind of the next morning, after breakfast, walking into my bedroom to find all three girls knitting with great focus.

Surprisingly, I must confess. I'm addicted. Though I've only begun a small scarf (Lesson One—start with only 26 stitches to avoid Long Tent Scarf Syndrome), I have found myself knitting whenever I can: in the car while my hubby drives, at the indoor beach resort while the kids swim, and right before bed to relax my mind. Knitting has been a surprising Memory Maker on several levels, including as a connector between grandmother, mother, and daughter, and as a gift that keeps on giving.

This season, I encourage you to create or experience one Memory Maker. Whether it be a craft, musical number, decorating diversion, or baked treat, do something special with your children to make the season particularly memorable.

Thankful for Memorable Moments

The holidays are upon us, and that means bring on the Memorable Moments–those experiences that create a unique and meaningful holiday experience.

A few years ago I started a Holiday Journal. Don't feel nauseated just yet, I'm not incredibly dutiful but enjoy the entries we've recorded. As I flipped through this journal the other day, I nostalgically relived the past few years. I fingered holiday menus crinkled and smudged with some kind of sauce stapled onto the pages, with kids' names written next to certain entrees that apparently they helped make (or were supposed to make, or hid and got out of making...). I remembered trips to neighboring cities for a Memory Maker instead of a gift-getter Christmas. And read about the Thanksgiving my husband and sons volunteered to, then delayed, making the holiday pies. Finally, the dessert went in the oven at 1 p.m., *on Thanksgiving Day*, which meant the turkey went in after, which meant we didn't eat until *seven o'clock that night.*

I remember that.

But my absolute favorite entry was the following one for Easter 2006, which I had to put in its unbelievable entirety:

"What a day. Prepped the night before for Easter beautifully—all groceries in, Sunday clothes laid out, the house clean all around, and Easter treats already bought and ready for assembling.

Then Sunday dawned. I felt terrible—exhausted, headache, hormone stuff. [Got up] and left for church but forgot to put the ham in the oven. It sat *on the counter*, prepped, for three hours, while the oven sat on, for three hours. This didn't register until the closing prayer at church. Then in Relief Society [women's church meeting], I was holding Sophie but her foot caught as I went past the lesson table and down went the beautiful flowers. On and on it went...

After returning home, I put on my PJs and told my husband, I'm going to bed. Then I heard [our son] come in the front door yelling, 'Hey, why did you forget me at church?' Yes, we had completely forgotten him, and didn't even know it until he came home, which was a good twenty minutes later. The lady that brought him home called from the [clergy's] office so now everyone knew we were loser parents...

The whole day went like that, just totally off. Although, the rolls were a hit and we talked of the Savior and the meaning of Easter, and the children enjoyed the baskets. But honestly, I couldn't wait until the children went down. They were like popcorn, crying, whining, fighting, and I thought, Heaven help me. THAT was our Easter..."

So I hope this holiday you won't try for a magazine cover experience, but rather, enjoy memorable moments that you'll talk about–and laugh about–for many holidays to come.

Are You Having a Keeper Christmas?

One year after receiving an early Christmas gift from a neighbor, I mentioned how quickly she had finished her Christmas gifts. Surprisingly, she didn't seem that happy, and merely gave a huge sigh of relief and said "I'm DONE!"

Too often, Christmas can become one Santa-sized to-do list, made without any ho-ho-ho (or even mistletoe). This year, I invite you to not just "get it done", but to make it a Keeper Christmas, one that you'll remember.

One woman shared with me a surprising Christmas service experience. For a Christmas giving project, she had handed out assignments to their immediate and extended family to try to fill a *few* boxes with clothing and food donations.

However, when all the family members met together, they had actually filled *nine big boxes* stuffed full of food, gifts, and holiday decorations.

She wrote, "It was so exciting. All 41 of us headed to this family's home. The emotions that took over when the family answered the door were overwhelming! The father had been out of work for some time and the mother was eight months pregnant. They had been expecting us but I don't think at the volume at which we came. My point of the story is not to pat our back, but after this many years, the kids still say, 'Remember when we took all those boxes to that family? Are we doing that again?' They don't remember what they got from Santa or anyone else that year, but they remember singing Christmas songs to a family in need. I keep that in mind when I think I need to buy 'just one more gift'..."

It's cliche but true; giving is so much better than getting, and much more of a keeper Christmas. Recently, when I asked my children what they received for Christmas three years ago, they

66

couldn't remember (and *their* memory cells are intact). But when we talked of past keeper moments the first thing they shared (and continue to share) is being the Secret Santa. They recalled years of dressing up in dad's big overcoat, then stealth-like waiting and approaching until the coast was clear to ring the doorbell.

Just like my friend, our family is helping a needy family this season too. Their simple wants include a pair of work shoes for the grandma, work pants for the mother, and diapers for the baby. It's been a humbling and poignant experience for our children to see the reality of people's lives, and what activities and experiences make a truly keeper Christmas.

When doing something for others isn't just a task on a list, it becomes a part of our individual and family history. This year, make it a Keeper Christmas with a focus on showing love and kindness to those in need.

Guess Who's Coming to Dinner

When a family member comes to visit, so can an added measure of anticipation and anxiety. As I considered how to combat that, the following ideas have proven happily successful.

1. Decide ahead of time a few major things you will do.

Before a family member came to visit, we sat down to family dinner and threw out suggestions of what we wanted to do. This was not uber planning, this was survival. With six children, if something isn't planned well, you can only imagine the "adventure" that awaits.

And on that note, mix up the age-focused activities so that it won't be endless McToyland or that you are playing 24/7 hostess. We finalize our schedule to include a few adult choices as taking my mother to a Christmas play; children choices such as cookie decorating; and family choices like going to Temple Square.

2. Do one major thing a day.

I am a chronic jam-packer who initially thinks, "Hey, that activity/event/overwhelming must-do sounds *really fun.*" Then after the second activity/event/must-do in an as many hours, I am *really a Grinch*. One major outing a day is plenty. The rest of the time can be spent in at-home activities or restful recuperation.

3. Consider your expectations.

Much of family contention comes from differing expectations on how the visit will go, what you will do and everything in between. A few years ago my mother came to visit after a several-year absence. I wasn't sure how to handle this best so I went for candid. I just emailed and said something like, This is how things run at our house with many children; after reading this if you're still game (and not in mortal fear) we hope you'll visit. This truly took the worry out of the unknown for me and also helped my mother know what to expect.

Along these same lines, it's important to recognize with family, you don't have to be chained at the hip to have a great experience. Letting people come and go, helping them know the schedule of when to return for vital events, is a very good thing. With the timing of my mother's visit, I still had some appointments that couldn't be changed. But wonderfully, this alone time with the children gave my mother more togetherness with the little ones. It also helped me to avoid backlogging errands avoiding a mountain of to-dos awaited me when she left.

A family visit requires a healthy mix of patience and candor. My mother surely had many things she wanted to share in the way of parenting tips, but she didn't. We were ourselves. We held no grudges. We truly enjoyed what was presented to us.

I think of the memories made during my mother's visit, and how our children will remember them. Ultimately, she gained discovery time with the children, reconnecting time with me, and a memorable time experienced together, to savor now and build on next time.

Let Go of the Cookie Cutter Christmas

As the days wind down to the final holiday event, we're assaulted by annoying slogans and questions; "Buy Now—80% Off!" and "Finished Your Shopping? Sale Ends Today!"

Or the worst one of all: "Ready for Christmas?"

Relax. What hasn't been done so far probably wasn't that crucial. And what remains that *is* vital can be done more happily with a few of the following ideas.

Savor the Season. Slow down, today, even right now. Delight in the simple pleasures—sparkling lights, irritating familiar carols, the fifth plate of gift cookies. These joyful bits come once a year and remind us to celebrate the season and appreciate the unexpected, and perhaps undesired.

Janene Wolsey Baadsgaard shares in *Families Who Laugh...Last* that one year she found her young daughter in the bathroom in the midst of hundreds of white paper pieces literally everywhere. Confused and in mother mode, Janene told her daughter to clean up the mess. Later, Janene understood the purpose of the mess after receiving a special Christmas gift—a homemade snow globe.

Can anyone say "mother guilt"?

So welcome what comes daily, especially the plentiful opportunities to lift someone's load. The other day while at breakfast with a friend we noticed a lady leaning on a walker. Spontaneously, we offered to help with her packages and she accepted. In those few minutes I felt a tangible joy from simply being available to help another. These are the experiences that make the holidays fulfilling.

Don't force the celebration. So the cookies burned, the pine tree died, or the person bringing the main dish didn't get the message. Live the dream anyway! Let down and be part of the experience without choreographing a superficially successful one. My husband and I host a company party each year. Because some of his floor installation crews speak a limited amount of English, sometimes I've worried if everyone is enjoying the evening.

However, this year I promised myself to stop stressing and start enjoying the people, even if it meant some awkward silence. And it was amazing! I was able to talk with a woman who had suffered polio as a child and now was able to walk with a crutch. She also volunteered for several organizations while studying filmmaking. Currently, a few of her documentary films on homelessness and domestic violence were being shown in homeless shelters. What a fabulous connection we enjoyed. I learned to let go of being the Stressed Out Happy Fairy (i.e., "IS EVERYBODY HAVING FUN?") and instead, be in the moment.

Give people the benefit of the doubt. Watching the play *A Christmas Carol*, I remembered a poignant comment on the story, which was this: that even though Scrooge had had a change of heart—as incredible as it was—that Cratchett's wife and Scrooge's nephew still had to frankly forgive him. Clearly, they were completely unaware as to what Scrooge had personally experienced. And yet, they welcomed his sudden change with open arms.

We can do that too. Even when a family member hasn't experienced a "mighty change of heart," that's okay. We can still let go of being irked at their choices and choose to love them for this season. Instead of becoming angry at familiar triggers, we can try a quick smile and change the conversation. Or, we can plan ahead for predictable choices (i.e. Uncle Bob is always late, Aunt Midge is typically bossy). And we can even let said Aunt Midge decorate the table as she likes—what does it matter in the long run? Just for now, we can open our arms and hearts without pre-conceived prejudices, and simply let people be.

71

As Christmas Day approaches, let's give ourselves permission to let go of the cookie cutter Christmas. Instead, let's revel in the carols, sample the baked goods, and appreciate the unexpected but profound before us.

Give the Meaningful Gift

Despite lack of time, energy, or planning (if you've put off holiday shopping as long as I have), a meaningful gift doesn't need to be stressful or time-consuming. It's about sharing the *real* you or blessing someone's life with a simple act. It's about gifts of forgiveness, love, or kindness (as in, *not* sending that sequined cowboy hat).

In the book, *Becoming a Better You*, author Joel Osteen shares the experience of a woman who was driving a brand new car when at an intersection she gets in an accident. Afterwards, and in tears, she tells the gentleman whose car she had hit that her car was a gift from her husband. As she reaches into the glove compartment she sees attached to the insurance information a note that says, "Honey, just in case you ever have an accident, please remember I love *you* and not the car."

These kinds of thoughtful, gentle gifts are priceless, and lasting. A few years ago when I came down with pneumonia, a neighbor brought by a grocery bag full of chick flicks and a book series called *At Home in Mitford*. Bringing books and movies can be a bold move because people's tastes are so different. But what made this more heartfelt was that she had been sick too, for a long time. By experience she knew what I would need for recovery: soothing and lovely images to distract me from the daily reality. That book series saw me through an intensely difficult time and has become a personal favorite.

Meaningful gifts often share a bit of who you are: your tastes, your joys, your talents. One lady chose to type and bind some of her favorite recipes and give them as gifts. My husband, before mass cell phones, bought gift phone cards for his family. That way he could call them whenever he wanted throughout the year. And one Christmas I hand-painted tree ornaments for all our extended family members (during a hotel overnighter, painting while watching all six episodes of *Pride and Prejudice*. That was a meaningful Christmas gift).

Instead of checking off a list, consider sharing something a tad more personal. Often, you'll find that a heartfelt gift won't involve things. Is there a friend you haven't spoken to because of unhealed differences? A family member you avoid, or a co-worker you can't stand? Perhaps this year, for just one month, you can give them the gift of love. Each time you see them say a silent, "I love you" in your mind, even if you don't feel it, even if just being in the same square footage makes you want to reach in and pull out their larynx. We can do anything for thirty days, right?

Personal presents take a little thought, and a bit of sacrifice, but that's exactly what makes them so treasured. Whether it's about a fender bender, forgiving someone, or sacrificing something important, perhaps our greatest joy this season will be giving the meaningful gift.

Create a Joyful Christmas

Remember what you received last year from Uncle Bob or Aunt Lulu? Or what you gave them? Maybe not. And that's good news, because this year you can! Using a few simple tips, you and I can create a more joyful Christmas.

Simplify traditions. As a woman, I unwittingly allow myself to be ruled by the Holiday Must-do Minutiae of "but we must have hollyhocks on the door by December 1st," as if some rabid reindeer would otherwise attack. By choosing a few simple traditions—not all of them—we keep the joy and avoid the frazzle. As a family, decide on three or four must-haves—doing Sub for Santa, viewing the downtown holiday lights, etc.—then rotate others through the next season. Do a family newsletter every other year and instead, send a photo postcard in between. Try a potluck Christmas Eve dinner—do the ham and let everyone or Costco pitch in the rest.

Or combine serving with other families. Our neighbors once organized a neighborhood Sub for Santa giving party to replace neighbor gifts—that's my kind of tradition. This kind of simplifying creates less stress and more connection.

Author James Scott Bell shares that to write well first, one has to go over-the-top in description and plot points then pull back twenty-five percent to make it just right. That's a pretty good life principle. Likely, we've all done the over-the-top Christmas—too much and too hurried. Try pulling back by a quarter and enjoy the new breathing room.

Say no. Kindly, lovingly, but firmly say, "I wish we could, but we won't be able to this year." If needed, practice in the mirror. The holidays can bring on the guilt because it's a time of serving—but serving includes your own family. Evaluate your particular situation and *adjust* accordingly. This year, respond to opportunities with a silent question: "Will this create a joyful Christmas for my family?" If not, say, "Try us next year," because next year might be different for you and your family.

One Christmas I was pregnant with my seventh child. At age forty-six. Even when I attempted to move quickly, it was slow—as in, sloth slow. Trying to keep the same schedule as previous years would not have been pretty. So we adjusted. We didn't do the 12 days of Christmas but did Secret Santa on Christmas Eve. We didn't do five different food drives—but we did one. As a family we still served but notched it down to match our increased family situation. And, saying no to some structured things left room for seeing immediate needs of others, to serve in the moment without racing through a line-up of events.

Try one of these tips a try to avoid the rush-rush and instead, enjoy the hush-hush of a more joyful season this year.

Small Sacrifices Make Christmas Memories

It's profound how often in our Christmas memories that a small sacrifice is remembered more readily, and emotionally, than any I-couldn't-wait-to-have gift. Mary Ellen Edmunds illustrates this beautifully in her book, *Love is A Verb*.

She shares about a young girl from sixth grade named Beatrice who had a "crooked back and heart trouble." Mary Ellen's mother would ask Mary Ellen about this girl—if she was playing with the other children and if anyone was spending time with her. They weren't. Eventually, Mary Ellen's mother asked her to visit Beatrice and bring one favorite toy as a gift. Like most children, Mary Ellen didn't want to do either. But reluctantly, she gave in and chose one of her true favorites, a numbers game.

About this Mary Ellen says, "It was not with a burning sense of charity that I put my numbers game in the sack with Charlotte's toys. But at the same time, I know it didn't occur to me that I could get another numbers game if I gave this one to Beatrice. I was really giving it away; this was a true sacrifice if not exactly a charitable one."

Mary Ellen and her mother traveled to a poorer section of town to bring the toy to Beatrice. She continues, "It caught me off guard when we pulled up in front [of her house]. 'Mom, it's so small!' 'I know.' 'How many live here?' 'They have nine children, I think.' We went in and it seemed like there were beds everywhere. There were no more than three rooms...I saw Beatrice in one of the beds, looking quite small and rather pale."

At that moment Mary Ellen's mother reminded her to give Beatrice the toy she had brought. Beatrice lit up, and expressed how she has always wanted one of those games, and immediately began to play it.

Mary Ellen recalls, "Something happened inside of me at that moment—something significant. I was too tough to let it show on the outside, but in my heart something very important and good was happening. I felt happy. I felt I'd done something that mattered. I felt close to Beatrice and close to my mom."

What a poignant holiday experience. This story made me evaluate my life, to look at what I could sacrifice this season, and repeatedly the thought hit me, it's my time and agenda. It's putting down what I'm so busily engaged in, no matter the nobility of it, to listen to and be with family, friends, and neighbors.

It's a sweet and good thought, but one that's tougher to put into practice. Later that very week my husband asked me and our four-year-old to drive up to Salt Lake with him so we could spend time together while he did work errands. I hesitated. That meant the other children would come home afterschool to no one there. And we were going to a Christmas party that night and I wanted their chores completed beforehand. And there was post-weekend laundry spilling from the laundry room. Within seconds, I had pragmatically added the negatives and said thanks, but not this time honey.

After a few minutes the thought came, I'm being too functional. So I reversed it and said Hang the plan, let's be together. A small sacrifice in the scheme of things I'm sure, but the three of us had a ball together.

Obviously I needed another lesson because later that night after the party, we came home and I was, again, being functional. I helped the children get ready for bed and then had family scripture time by the tree. After singing Silent Night, someone jokingly suggested we sleep around it, under the lights. Although hesitating, for a while I did. But after half an hour I went upstairs and, very functionally, did my make-up routine, put on my pajamas, and climbed into our chilly bed, alone.

Again, a thought came: the whole family is downstairs and you're up here, alone, being functional. So I padded downstairs and couched it with my little one. Sure my husband and I were sore in the morning. But it was a memory maker, all of us sleeping in the family room, by the fire, under the pretty twinkling lights of the tree—a small insignificant sacrifice that at the very least, I'll remember.

So this Christmas, consider the small "sacrifices" you can offer your family or friends, ones they may not even know. But you will. And that feeling will bring the spirit of the season more fully into your soul.

New Year, Fabulous You

Years ago I faced a fresh calendar year and announced to myself: "I'm creating the Year of the Change!" Previous to this declarative moment, I had had four wonderful but energetic children, ages six and under. Emotionally, I was one step from the straight jacket, and physically, I resembled a bloated rutabaga, which was not good.

To move this changing quest forward, I asked myself four questions: What's working? What's not working? What do I want to do differently? How can I make it happen?

Using the answers as the basis for the year, I chose to lose weight first, focusing on gaining energy and vitality. I purchased a doable workout system and home gym, and hired a sitter occasionally to make it happen. Without crash diets or scary timelines, I dropped four sizes and for the first time in several years I truly felt fit and fabulous.

Ironically, while losing weight I experienced an incredible domino effect. My ability to focus on a healthy, positive goal now resulted in more overall self-control, energy, and clarity of thought. I felt more clarity with my feelings, laughed more spontaneously, and savored more fully my relationships. Through appropriately weight loss, I was also able to gain what I had hoped for, and much more.

I invite you to answer those four questions above for whatever isn't working for you. Try something new, different, and that has to do with those four questions. And remember to fully embrace the process of achieving them. This is your year to be and do just what you have always hoped and dreamed.

3 Quick Changes for the New Year:

Sometimes as women we suffer from Perfection Paralysis (at the New Year, after a women's conference, on Mother's Day, just to name a few). We're suddenly overwhelmed with feelings that we should be on the ball with x, y or z. And when we're not, we then simply avoid that x, y or z.

But we don't have to! Taking small chunks, making a few adjustments, or eliminating a negative behavior can jumpstart change, bypassing the inevitable paralysis that oversized goals can bring.

1) Get Organized: Begin with a Clean Counter. Although this is a down and dirty de-clutter, you focus on a doable area. First, take a look at the counter as is—with the backpacks, apple cores, soccer cleats, messy school papers, and strewn bills. Breathe. Now, visualize how you want the counter to really function: Do you need a file holder for kids' school info,? A phone stand and pad for scheduling? A billing center or holder for vital financial papers? Or fun family pictures to perk the whole look?

Next, take a large empty tub and put everything—every last bit of mess—into the tub. Voila. A clear counter. Lastly, only put back on the counter what belongs. If you can, add those decorative touches that might be missing—pretty colored containers or a bushy plant. Now step back, have a sasparilla, and enjoy the beauty.

2) Get Fit & Fabulous. Lose a habit, Get a habit. It's that simple. To eliminate a habit, try cutting just 100 calories a day— doing so, you could lose ten pounds in a year. That means baked chips instead of fried (saves 150 calories), sandwiches wrapped in a lettuce leaf instead of bread (about 150), or opting for two slices

81

of wheat toast over that innocent looking bagel (a big 200). If you're feeling brave, kick your soda intake for the day. A typical American sucks down 200 calories of sugary soda daily. Eliminate it and you can lose two pounds in a month with that one change.

To *get* a habit, try *brief* exercise to lose 100 calories a day. Just three minutes of jumping jacks with one or two pound weights, doing 100 without stopping, will sculpt arms and cut the calories.

Or, try adding just one fruit or vegetable per meal—just one. So doable, both new habits are quick and easy to assimilate. Combine a few "lose and get habits" and drop weight even faster!

3) Get Financially Set: Do a Money Hunt. As a family (kids love this), go through the house and find spare change. Pair children in teams and make it a contest of who can find the most, and first—it's hysterical, enlightening, and lucrative (one time we found seventy-five dollars in the house, no small change.) Depending on your family's needs and focus, put the money toward a family financial goal or donate it to charity, etc. Next, Money Hunt in your family budget. Again, make it a game—split into teams and see who can brainstorm how to save the most money in the budget.

I've found that if I "shop at home" I can save big. That means one week of the month I don't buy anything but dairy and simply "shop" from our cabinets, fridge, and freezer. I regularly have saved around two hundred to three hundred dollars a month from that one change (disclaimer: we have big-appetite teenage boys).

Give one of these jumpstart tips a try and see just how doable making changes can be.

Out of Hibernation and Into the New Year

Most of us come out of our holiday caves in cranky hibernating-bear mode, blinking and whining, "Already?"

But this year, I invite you to jump out of your cave, beat your chest, and bellow something inspiring like, "*I'm alive, and so are you!*" Then begin the rapturous journey of living, loving, and learning during the next twelve fresh, clean-slate months to become what you really, truly want to become.

If you're still hovering between the "cranky bear" and "I'm alive" stages, consider your values and how your life is aligned with them.

Think for a minute about your personal life wheel. What is the hub, the core of what makes you roll along daily, the substance of what matters most to you? Have you taken minutes yet to get quiet and think about what your ideal life could look like this coming year?

Part of values is spiritual direction, whatever that looks like to you. So I encourage you to be still and let what I call "feeling-thoughts" surface. As they do, write them down without self-editing.

I did this exercise with 3 x 5 notecards. As I allowed myself to brainstorm the coming year and what it could look like, several thoughts came (i.e. be still daily for thirty minutes, stay organized, and replace severe chocolate craving at 3 p.m. with yoga.). I simply wrote them one at a time on the cards. Then I organized the cards into three main areas—Self, Relationships, and Life Skills. Each of these life areas are like the wheel spokes. I could see that as I addressed and strengthened each wheel spoke, I could balance the turning of the wheel in my personal progression.

Try that same brainstorm exercise and see what thoughts come to you. And remember, after doing so, it could be tempting to overwhelm yourself with all your desired changes at once. To avoid this, sort through the cards and only choose *the top three areas* that resonate with your mind and soul.

Then choose the *top ONE* want-to-do in each area. *Lastly, look for the number one life area (i.e. get fit, get organized, etc.) that gives the most knock-your-socks off, let's-get-changing feeling.* Definitely begin with that one. In that life area do one goal, each week, even just for ten minutes at a time to keep moving forward.

As you complete this life exercise, focus your energy, and plan wisely, a peace and fulfillment will flow through your life. Your daily enjoyment will increase and your ability to cull out the unnecessary will be sharpened. Quite simply, your quality of life will markedly improve because you will clearly know what will make you and those you love truly happy.

This year, consider what matters most to you, then put your *best* energy into those areas, starting with the most vital. Begin with a clear focus of values, purpose, and inspiration, then apply appropriate energy and enjoy the journey. Here is to discovering and developing a deeper you.

Bonus Excerpts from
Faithful, Fit & Fabulous and
Create a Powerful Life Plan: 3 Simple Steps to Your Ideal Life

If you're looking for a fresh start for the new year, check out *Faithful, Fit & Fabulous* and the jumpstart personal program to achieve 8 goals in 8 weeks in 8 life areas: Holy Habits, Create a Life Plan, Joy in Womanhood, Fit & Fabulous, Get Organized, Balance Womanhood & Motherhood, Create Healthy Relationships, Establish Financial Peace and Prosperity.

And, if you desire to get back to center with more clarity in your life direction, enjoy *Create a Powerful Life Plan: 3 Simple Steps to Your Ideal Life*. In these clear steps you will create a mini blueprint of your ideal life so you can start living it.

Simple, doable, enjoyable. Make this *your* year for change with these fabulous books!

Faithful, Fit & Fabulous
Chapter 3: Joy in Womanhood

In speaking with women over the past 15 years, I hear conflicting information from women on ability to have joy. Some feel it's selfish to spend time on oneself, that free time should be spent just on serving. Other women hesitate to develop talents, achieve goals, or fulfill dreams, feeling that it isn't allowed. Some women wait for others—a spouse or a good friend—to give them permission to feel joy.

More of these "Joy Drainers" are rooted in worries, distractions, and perceived imperfections. Sister Sheri Dew once said that we are baited with temporal pleasures and preoccupations including our bank accounts, wardrobes, and waistlines. He is very aware that where our earthly treasure is, there will our hearts be also.

Each of the reasons for not feeling joy have one thing in common—they can be changed. Add a few "Joy Juicers"—mental and daily shifts—and you *can* feel excited about your life.

Joy Juicer #1: Be Yourself, Be Your Best Self

We're all unique. Some say weird, others say different, but these words generally mean the same thing: "not like me." We tend to be like seventh-graders: spending our time at recess looking for someone to be with, to say we're not alone, we're not rejected. This concept is what causes grown women to walk to the bathroom together.

Rejoice in your uniqueness, or weirdness, despite how others make you feel. We can celebrate our particular traits and behaviors because God wants and needs diversity. My friend's family loves pickles on their pizza. Another friend enjoys creating food storage recipes with beans. I get giddy in an office supply store. No two women's traits will be alike, so thoroughly enjoy what makes you creatively you.

Female religious leader Patricia T. Holland has said, "The Lord uses us *because* of our unique personalities and differences rather than in spite of them. He needs every one of us, with all our blemishes and weaknesses and limitations." (Patricia T. Holland, "Filling the Measure of Our Creation," in *On Earth as It Is in Heaven*, Salt Lake City: Deseret Book, 1989, page 6).

When we're unhappy, we've likely looked in the wrong direction—sideways rather than upward. In this competitive world, we women can be our own worst enemies. When someone has said something unkind or made you feel insignificant, it doesn't have to rock your world. Respond instead by going to your Father in Heaven to know what He thinks.

Author and religious leader Chieko Okazaki shares a profound experience with this very concept. After moving from Hawaii, she planned to teach at an elementary school in Utah. Because it wasn't long after World War II and Sister Okazaki was of Japanese descent, she prepared for possible racism. A few days before school started, the principal told Sister Okazaki that three mothers requested their children be transferred out of her class.

How would you respond to this?

She didn't take it personally and went about plans for the first day. She shares:

"It could have been a threatening situation. I could have chosen to feel frightened and let the children and parents feel that. Or I could have chosen to be ultra-stern and rigidly professional by way of covering that up. But what I wanted the children to feel was my own joy and excitement."

Rather than hide, she made an exotic-colored dress with a matching flower tucked in her hair. Assembling her first class she could feel their excitement and anticipation.

Later, the principal called Sister Okazaki and mentioned that the three mothers had now asked to have their children reinstated in her class. The principal said, "I told them, 'opportunity knocks only once.'" (Chieko Okazaki, *Lighten Up*, Salt Lake: Deseret Book, 1993, 49-50).

Celebrate your unique qualities and let them bless the lives of others.

Joy Juicer #2: Have Fun!

That's right, I used the word "fun." About you. When was the last time you had fun? My stake president says that if we're not having fun living the gospel, we're not doing it right.

A few years ago, I carved out some time to go to a bookstore (my place of fun) for about an hour. While exiting the store, I heard the loudspeaker say something like, "Fresh out of the oven, our hot, lemon blueberry scones. Stop by the bakery and try one." They got me. Even though I'm not a scone fan, I salivated. Running to the counter, I nabbed one of those fresh, hot scones and hopped in the car to feast on the drive home. It was out of this world! Melt-in-your-mouth warm goodness with a cold bottle of milk—it was so delicious that I had to call my husband. I told him it was utterly delicious and lamented not buying one for him (as I licked my fingers).

Years ago I remember my preschool son earned the consequence of washing our tiny bathroom floor. After putting in a load of wash, I came back and saw him swirling the cloth in the bucket, splashing and making airplane noises, and generally having a great time. In typical mom mode, I put my hands on my hips and said sternly, "This isn't playtime—you're to do your consequence." With the words hanging in the air, I started laughing. Totally ridiculous! If he wants to have fun with a consequence, kudos to him.

Have fun. Every single day. Pamper yourself, be gentle with yourself, do something nice for yourself. Life can be hard and appreciation scarce, so do something lovely. What about no chores on Friday? Or stop housekeeping duties after 6 p.m.? Perhaps "Mom's Time" after 9 p.m.? I've used each one, and they have been *fun*.

Obviously I'm not talking uber spa queen, going to an extreme where life becomes all about you. I'm talking about good, old-fashioned, everyday happy things. Someone once suggested to make a list of activities you like doing, and activities you feel good after doing.

For example, "like doing" might be: take a nap, read a book, or go to lunch with a friend. "Feel good after doing," might include working out, baking something your family loves, or cleaning out a closet—initially it may not seem fun, but afterward you feel great. Case in point—have you ever cleaned a closet, and then walked past it again, saying, "Wow, that's a good-looking closet"? That's fun!

Back to Basics—Go!

List five things you like to do and five things you feel good after doing.

Like Doing	Feel Good After Doing
1.	1.
2.	2.
3.	3.
4.	4.
5.	5.

Now try one this week and feel the joyful change begin!

[Excerpt from *Faithful, Fit & Fabulous: Get Back to Basics and Transform Your Life in 8 Weeks*, Connie Sokol, Vyne Publishing). Available on Amazon or www.conniesokol.com.

Create a Powerful Life Plan: 3 Simple Steps to Your Ideal Life!

Chapter 1: My Successful Life Change:
From Housewife Slug to Happy Hot Mama!

What do you want?

This is the second scariest question a woman can face, only slightly better than, "How much do you weigh?" If you are like most people, this question will invite a blank stare and let-me-see-back-in-1985 stories. But knowing what you want is crucial. , Without that, you will never get what you want, be happy with what you have, or savor what comes your way.

Not knowing is a tough way to fly.

What began *my* what-do-I-want journey was having four children in six years. At that point, my energy and most likely my brain cells were completely spent. At the start of the seventh year some energy returned—an inexplicable burst, in fact, during which I announced, "I LIVE!"—but it was more like the energy of a marathoner taking her last step before she's declared legally dead. Nevertheless, I was determined. My husband and I rang in the New Year waving our banner (okay, *my* banner), "The Year of Change." This had nothing to do with menopause and everything to do with finally setting goals and getting my life in balance. Pumped, juiced, smoothied, I made my plan, tacked it on the wall, and said with great gusto, "Big Mama is back!"

And then I forgot. Or maybe I should say that I slowly faded back into what I call "The Haze," where first you think about accomplishing your goals, then avoid thinking about your goals, and finally end with "What goals? I am woman, I am acceptable," and scarfing a king-size Kit Kat. Bottom line: I had zero life. Meanwhile between snacks I had hired a babysitter for a few hours each week to take the children while I went upstairs and did something somewhat enjoyable, although unproductive those rare times I could even remember what enjoyable was.

My epiphany came when on such a day I went upstairs, closed the door, and threw on the bed a remote control, a grocery list, a few books, and a goal list. I stared at them—totally devoid of emotion, and suddenly I wanted a Kit-Kat. Then uncharacteristically I turned on a daytime TV channel (since during kid "business hours" viewing was pretty much limited to *Blue's Clues*). A popular daytime talk show happened to be on, and women of all ages and experiences were sharing how they had been searching for answers about life and its challenges, where they fit in the universe, and much more.

So here I was watching this show with women asking questions I knew could be answered. I also knew the answers that could make them happy, and suddenly it hit me that I had something to offer. That was that. A surge of part frustration, part Big Mama welled within, and I defiantly turned off the TV, turned to the bookcase, and loudly shouted, "WHAT DO YOU WANT?" At that point I was, first of all, thankful for sturdy wall insulation, and second, fed up with my Twinkie life (looks good on the outside, no recognizable substance on the inside).

I ripped out a piece of paper and wrote in gashing letters across the top, "WHAT DO YOU WANT?" Not stopping to think about *proper* answers, I wrote furiously, straight from the gut: "Write a book, speak to women, sing, feel healthy" and more. Then, after only a slight pause, I turned over the paper and just as feverishly wrote, "What is stopping me?"

I watched my pencil confirm what my gut had been trying to tell me, but what I hadn't wanted to know: "Spending too much time on husband's business, lazy about my dreams, not making this a priority in my life," and on and on. Sitting back for a breath, I looked at my work. There squeezed onto only two pages of paper was probably the equivalent of three years of therapy. I felt clean, purged, and ready for action.

After sifting and arranging thoughts, praying and thinking, eating and pondering, I knew trying to achieve all of my goals at once would be overwhelming. My new mantra was to choose one thing and see it to completion. So I chose losing weight first because, basically, I hated looking like a bloated turnip. Not wanting to become skinny-focused, however, I decided to first lose some habits: emotional eating, obsessing about weight, checking my thighs ten times a day, and other undisciplined behaviors.

This moment was big (no pun intended). For the first time in years I determined, truly determined, to have a healthy body and spend only the necessary time thinking about it. But more than that, I was focused on changing my whole life, and hoping to do it one step at a time.

I paid attention to people and ideas that reflected my goals. I cut out and posted on the wall a picture of a woman's body I knew mine could resemble without bizarre and drastic surgery. I got specific and realistic about exercise. Regularly hitting the gym was not an option because I had four little ones at home, but I found a body-changing program that I felt would work. After some negotiation, my husband and I bought free weights and took "before" pictures that made me cry.

I had my ups and downs. In the beginning, after four straight weeks of being "so good," I looked even fatter and wanted to cry. No, I wanted a really big cheesecake. But I hung in there and the very next week the weight started to come off like a fake sumo suit. Meanwhile, the kids got repeatedly sick, my husband's workload increased ridiculously, and I injured myself slightly (although with much complaint). Throughout the setbacks, I kept at it, seeing my goal to completion.

I noticed a startling domino effect. Because of what I was learning from my physical transformation—discipline, patience, and endurance, all just from controlling the chocolate intake—I quickly began to feel more self-control in other areas of my life. I had more energy and more clarity of thought. I felt more in tune with my feelings. I knew when I wanted and needed to write, to sing, to laugh out loud, or spend an overnighter with my husband. My thinking expanded as I freed myself from self-imposed limitations.

I returned to motivational speaking and a few years later, restarted an organization on the side to help strengthen families. From these experiences and research, I created a program to help women change their lives. This book shares the Life Plan component to help you change your life, too.

Using this book I'll take you through the three simple steps of creating your very own Life Plan, which will serve as a blueprint for your ideal life. The Life Plan will help you discover your life purposes and desires, and then help you determine specific steps to achieve them.

What is a Life Plan? It gives you that starting point, pulling together the thoughts, dreams, desires, and want-to-dos from your head, and getting them down in an organized fashion on paper. This small but powerful principle works. Over the years with my Life Plan—and help from above—I've been able to write and publish books, be a national and local speaker, lose and keep off twenty-five pounds (after seven pregnancies!), become more spiritually grounded, stay close to my children and teach them life skills, make and save money, travel, be a TV and radio host, and in general, create a more loving harmonious home (the latter is up for debate).

This is a process of clarifying what you really, truly want from life, right now, and in the future. This clarity helps you decide how you'll spend your time, energy, and resources. And those choices will yield specific results.

David Allen, author of *The Art of Getting Things Done* says, "Thinking in a concentrated manner to define desired outcomes is something few people feel they have to do. But in truth, outcome mimics reality."

If you create a positive, inspired life plan, you will undoubtedly accomplish it, in some way, at some time, in your life. That's what's so amazing. Time and tide is on your side.

Let's get started.

[From *Create a Powerful Life Plan: 3 Simple Steps to Your Ideal Life*, Connie Sokol, Vyne Publishing.] Available on Amazon or www.conniesokol.com.

More Books From Connie Sokol

If you're not sure which to choose or where to begin, try the category you're most interested in.

Start a life change:
Faithful, Fit & Fabulous (faith-based)
Create a Powerful Life Plan

Inspirational:
40 Days with the Savior (faith-based)
Motherhood Matters (faith-based)
Faithful, Fit & Fabulous (faith-based)

Just for fun
The Life is Too Short Collection
Caribbean Crossroads (romance)

All titles are available as ebooks and print books at www.amazon.com or www.conniesokol.com.

Faithful, Fit & Fabulous: Get Back to Basics and Transform Your Life in 8 Weeks! (A simple life-planning, goal-setting system that helps moms tidy up 8 life areas in 8 weeks)

http://www.amazon.com/Faithful-Fit-Fabulous-Transform-ebook/dp/B005Z4CGDK/ref=sr_1_2?ie=UTF8&qid=1381964726&sr=8-2&keywords=connie+sokol

Create a Powerful Life Plan: 3 Simple Steps to Your Ideal Life (A step-by-step guide to creating a Life Plan that works)

http://www.amazon.com/Create-Powerful-Simple-Steps-ebook/dp/B00AY7P6M6/ref=sr_1_3?ie=UTF8&qid=1381964726&sr=8-3&keywords=connie+sokol

The Life is Too Short Collection—Kitchen Table Wisdom with a Side of Humor (A collection of the most-loved columns from the "Life Is Too Short" series)

http://www.amazon.com/Life-Too-Short-Collection-ebook/dp/B00C3976H6/ref=sr_1_4?ie=UTF8&qid=1381964726&sr=8-4&keywords=connie+sokol

40 Days with the Savior—A Daily Devotional Book to Draw Closer to Christ (A daily thought on 40 character traits of Jesus Christ and how they can apply in the life of a woman, wife, and mother)

http://www.amazon.com/40-Days-Savior-ebook/dp/B00BI4278K/ref=sr_1_1?ie=UTF8&qid=1381964726&sr=8-1&keywords=connie+sokol

Motherhood Matters: Joyful Reminders of the Divinity, Reality, and Rewards of Motherhood-(A gift book)

http://www.amazon.com/Motherhood-Matters-Reminders-Divinity-ebook/dp/B007TY9HW2/ref=sr_1_7?ie=UTF8&qid=1381964726&sr=8-7&keywords=connie+sokol

Caribbean Crossroads-(An award-nominated romance and #1 on Amazon Kindle)

http://www.amazon.com/Caribbean-Crossroads-Connie-E-Sokol-ebook/dp/B0089SWBTS/ref=sr_1_6?ie=UTF8&qid=1381964726&sr=8-6&keywords=connie+sokol

 ABOUT THE AUTHOR

Connie Sokol is a mother of seven, a national and local presenter, and a favorite speaker at Education Week. She is the Motherhood Matters contributor on KSL TV's "Studio 5 with Brooke Walker", and a regular blogger for KSL "Motherhood Matters" on www.ksl.com. She is a former TV and radio host for Bonneville Communications, and columnist for *Deseret News* and *Utah Valley Magazine*.

Mrs. Sokol is the author of several books including *The Life is Too Short Collection, Faithful, Fit & Fabulous, Motherhood Matters, Create a Powerful Life Plan, 40 Days with the Savior,* and *Caribbean Crossroads.* Mrs. Sokol marinates in time spent with her family and eating decadent treats. She welcomes comments, questions, and experiences regarding the book's content at me@conniesokol.com. For her blog, TV segments, podcasts and more, visit www.conniesokol.com.